GW00506533

"WARS ARE WOT YOU MAKE 'EM!"

Published by Wolfgang Publishing,
Wings, Court Street, Winsham
Chard, Somerset, TA20 4JE

Printed by Rapid Print, Chard

Copyright Paul A. Smith

ISBN 0 9524892 1 X

"Wars are wot you make 'em!"

by
Paul A. Smith

Wolfgang Publishing

Illustrations are from line drawings done at the time or specially drawn by me for the book.

A survival story of how to avoid becoming cannon fodder. By a fit country lad of nineteen who was highly allergic to footdrill, bullshit of all sorts and the Sergeant Majors who arranged it.

The story covers 6½ years and deals with 'The Phoney War', The Battle of Britain, College Life, Radar Schools, Touring around Scapa Flow in the Orkneys, 'D' Day, The General Election and Demob.

The theme is that, even in an army in Wartime, it is possible to remain master of one's own destiny.

Chapter list

Dedicated to
MONICA

CHAPTER ONE
THE LAST KILL

The animal was crouching motionless in the dark circle of trampled grass around the wooden peg that held the snare. The shiny copper wire bit deeply into the tortured skin of its neck; its head so swollen that its eyes were popping out and its mouth hung open gasping for breath. What we rabbit catchers called a 'strangler' - worth only 4d. Most snares gave a 'clean' kill - a broken neck, and that meant 6d.

I bent down, grabbed its back legs and held it up ready for the chop behind the ears that would cause instant death to another rabbit. I raised my right hand, fingers straight ... I hesitated.

Although I thought that rabbits were only second to fish in their unfeeling stupidity, I felt compelled to let this one go. This day, 3rd September 1939, was different. Looking round furtively to see that no one watched my strange behaviour, I picked the sliding noose from the neck. Put down again, the rabbit resumed its position on the grass - long since resigned to death. Rabbits didn't seem to mind dying.

Picking the rabbit up I quickly walked over to the hedge and pushed it towards a burrow and safety. As it slowly moved away a gentle rustling in my coat pocket reminded me that I was not the only creature interested in death. Alerted by

The Snare

1

the merest smell of blood Pogey, my pet ferret, was peering up at me with his pink eyes, his red tongue licking across his needle-sharp teeth.

He had helped me catch hundreds of rabbits, bolted from their holes into my purse nets. His reward was a warm bit of guts and liver from a newly killed rabbit; still steamy hot and wriggling before the nerve had died. He had been my constant hunting companion and was completely fearless - rabbits, stoats, weasels and rats fled before him so that I, and my lurcher dog called Spring, could make a kill. Spring had not learnt to avoid snares so he was not with us.

I had left school early during the farming depression of the 1930s and as my only reward for working long hours on the small family farm - mostly hand milking, mucking out and hedge cutting - I was appointed the rabbit catcher in my spare time. My small team of Pogey, Spring and I could - with snares, traps, nets and a small bore rat-gun - keep pests at bay and I could sell skins, rabbits, wild fruits and mushrooms for pocket money. We three ate a lot of meat and were a good match for the foxes, badgers and poachers than abounded in the hills of South Somerset. I was self reliant, toughened by the vagaries of the weather - and happy.

As War clouds gathered in early 1939 I found that the Territorial Army would pay my travel expenses to Taunton for two hourly evening sessions a week and a sort of holiday at a Dartmoor Artillery Camp. I joined the Artillery as all Somerset villages had their War Memorials and a sprinkling of scarred and prematurely old men who had returned from being in the Infantry in the Great War.

This day was 3rd September 1939. I had heard Neville Chamberlain's 'We are now at War with Germany' over the wireless. I felt numb and shocked. In the afternoon I was collecting all my snares so that I could become a full time soldier in the morning. At nineteen years of age I realised that I was probably unlikely to survive another War.

Pogey

My observation of the Army so far was that nothing much had changed over the years... it was a complete contrast to farming. We had so little equipment that we just did a bit of basic drill, pushed around two 18 Pounder Howitzers and listened to a few lectures. As a recruit I only had overalls, no uniform - and certainly no weapons - our two old Howitzers were highly polished and used for ceremonial purposes and a little drill. I found the Army a very strange organisation.

With the outbreak of War all reserves were ordered to report to their Units but the Yeomanry were given an extra day as no one worked on a Sunday. I was,

2

Into line

they told me, to be called up as a fully trained soldier but I would be of little use - unless they wanted a Regimental rabbit catcher or perhaps even a poacher.

So my last home job was to clear up my rabbit snares planted the previous day. As I reached my last field I had a dozen carcasses threaded on to a carrying stick and the snares, with their pegs and holders, at one end.

I was now nearly at the top of the farm and the final gateway. From my vantage point I could see for miles down the River Axe valley with the sea glinting through a gap in the cliffs nearly twenty miles away at Seaton. The fields were verdant green with the September grass still springy under foot and the trees were still rounded, lush and friendly. The grass was still actively growing and the rabbits made well-marked runs out from their holes in the woodside hedge to their nightly eating patches in mid field.

Pogey was lying quietly in my old jacket pocket as I hurried on looking for dead or dying snared rabbits and the untouched snares still pegged and positioned out into the runs. Some were difficult to see but I would not be able to be back again so all must be collected.

Suddenly I stumbled, my left foot firmly held in a snare that I had failed to spot. I fell forwards throwing the stick of carcasses around me. Pogey had been woken up and in a few seconds had left my pocket and was fastening his teeth into the nearest rabbit; it was shaking and squealing with delight. I knew how disgraceful is was for a trapper to get caught in his own traps. To make matters worse I had fallen with one hand in a cow pat and another gripping a very angry thistle. It was at this point that I realised that we were being watched.

"Ullow young man! Be zaying your prayers - or zummit?"

I did not need to look up at the source of the gruff voice. Old Gaarge worked on the next farm, when he wasn't poaching pheasants. He had little use for youngsters, especially farmers' sons, and was obviously enjoying my predicament.

"I'm - er...er... collecting - er... my catch - er - I'm away in the morning. The Army -" I volunteered

Wars... young man...

this last bit in case he would think I was going to a ballet school. I was by this time balancing on one leg and with waving arms trying desperately to release

3

the noose from by boot.

"Aaaah -" said the old man thoughtfully, "like us did in fourteen - you knowed what 'appened to a lot of us." His gnarled left hand rested on the top of the gate and he tapped the gate thoughtfully with his shepherd's crook. "Them's wot's names is on the memorial - them is, I reckon, the lucky ones."

I was gathering up the rabbits and, despite the attentions of Pogey trying to thread them again on my carrying stick. "Not all the younger men went off, did they?"

"Most of the more stupid ones volunteered - they was in first, Aaaah! Others replaced 'em if they was deaded." His beady little eyes peered out from his whiskery face and his well-patched hat.

"But some never went. They were called up - was it the medical?" I could see that Old Gaarge was treating this conversation as his last duty to the condemned.

"'Twas the draaft" he hesitated before telling me about this rumoured village secret. "You 'eard a bit about it - I expect? The draaft."

"Yes, the hemlock - was that it?" Most villagers whispered about the 'hemlock' tea drunk by reluctant recruits.

"Aaaah, gave 'em a bad 'eart - made 'em proper bad it did. 'Course they mended when they was sent back 'ome. Some of 'em were that near to call up that they nicknamed 'em 'Soldier' or 'Sailor' even after the War ended - they did. But many did come back -and it was the flu that got them then. Most either 'ad the gas - or the wood - or the metal though."

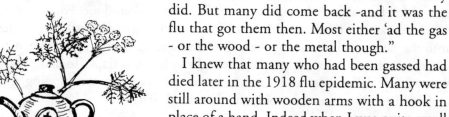

The 'Draaft'

I knew that many who had been gassed had died later in the 1918 flu epidemic. Many were still around with wooden arms with a hook in place of a hand. Indeed when I was quite small my mother used to use 'him with the 'hook' as a bogey man when I was very naughty. Most of the rest twitched as they walked for the jagged pieces of shrapnel were still in their bodies.

"What about you?" I asked, "You got through all right?" Gaarge was said to have been a batman or servant to a senior Officer and thus escaped the trenches. My father reckoned old Gaarge was as crafty as a 'cart load of monkeys'. It was old Gaarge who taught me how to lay snares - and told me to scent my hands with aniseed. It was some time later that I discovered that this smell was irresistible to foxes and stray dogs - leaving Gaarge's own snares untouched.

4

"Aaaah. You got to look after yerself in the Army - they bastards will get 'e killed if they can - you want to watch out young man. You don't want to be as dead as they bunnies - you want to be craafty - like that old ferret of yours"

I had now got all my rabbits gutted and threaded on my carrying stick. Pogey was fed and peered sleepily out of my pocket. I turned to go down the valley back home.

"Well I will be seeing you sometime - again," I said hopefully. I somehow felt that it wouldn't have greatly worried the old man if I did not come back.

He thought a moment, and slowly nodded his head. I sensed that he was trying to impart some piece of wisdom to me. "You got to look out to yerself in the Army."

As I walked away with the row of corpses he shouted his final bit of advice.

"Remember young man - Wars be wot you make 'em."

It was nearly a mile down the valley to the farmstead. It had been a hard life on the farm but now everything about seemed lovely. Although my arms ached I did not rest but hurried on. Then I passed the little stream and the high growth of purple stemmed hemlock with its faint musty smell.

The dead rabbits now appeared as soldiers on my stick - in line, unthinking - and very dead. Pogey had the best of life - well fed and when not out hunting in his warm cage with his mate. In the morning I would go into an unknown world. I somehow knew that a Wartime Army would be full of snares.

CHAPTER TWO

THE FIRST DAY:
4TH SEPTEMBER, 1939

The War started on a Sunday, which was a day of rest. So the West Somerset Yeomanry had asked us to report for an early start on the Monday. But this did not prove a very popular day for starting a war either, for when I arrived at the Taunton Barracks at about 10 o'clock that morning - having bid a tearful farewell to both humans and livestock on the Farm - only four other members of the Battery had turned up. One was the Battery Clerk, who had deserted his normal job at Taunton's railway station, and who was sitting at a trestle table in solitary state in the Battery Office with a long list of names - and a good book. Two others had been given a pickaxe handle each, and positioned either side of the entrance gate to the Territorial Barracks. They were told to salute all officers and not let other ranks out again to escape back into the Town. One just sighed 'Flippin Hell' as I went through. I did not know whether this was a commentary on my stupidity in arriving early or just his view of Wars; probably both. As I approached the clerk, resplendent in his new uniform with two stripes, he slowly put his book down and looked up as if I were about to buy a ticket.

"Gunner Smith 758," I said, perhaps vainly hoping that he would have actually greeted me. He slowly ticked me off the list in the best Great Western Railway style without actually looking at me.

"Better wait in the yard." He beckoned me to join our fourth member sitting on his kitbag. This fellow was obviously not of the warrior class either. This

7

was, after all, the first War we had started.

"I reckon we're the silly buggers - turning up early. Been sitting here two fucking hours already." He didn't even raise his eyes as he gazed despondently at the tarmac.

The yard was otherwise empty. My kit bag contained my entire stock of military equipment, most of which I had the privilege of purchasing myself: One towel, a spare set of underclothes, my overalls, toiletries, a very large tin of 'Blanco' and a 'Housewife'(pronounced Husif). So called because this small roll of needles, cotton and sundry mending equipment was, I was told, the nearest thing I would get to feminine care during War service. Also, in accordance with old farming traditions, I'd included a piece of wire, some string and a few nails. This made my kit bag not only lumpy but possibly hazardous to sit on.

My companion gave another sigh. "I reckon they Town buggers won't turn up till dumpsy - How far you come from then?"

"Twenty miles - there's only Infantry around my way." I replied.

Perhaps he came from a village too and did not relish the mud, bullets and the bayonets. "Same my way," he volunteered.

The War seemed not to make very much progress, for after another hour there were only six of us in the trap, just like rabbits waiting for a ferret.

And then 'General' turned up in a new uniform with the new single stripe of a Lance Bombardier. We at last had a leader.

The thought of war

During my six months association with the Territorials - including a fortnight on Dartmoor - I had learnt a little about the Army hierarchy.

The Officers were very remote and seemed only to function as figure heads. And most certainly never discussed matters with mere gunner recruits. They had worn uniforms - they had to buy their own. Below them were a motley collection of other ranks - ranging from a Battery Sergeant Major - known as a Permanent Staff Instructor - sundry sergeants and bombardiers. We newer gunners then wore overalls over our own clothes, which was very convenient as we would become civilians before we even left the parade ground, often much to the consternation of sundry drill sergeants - this operation may have been the origin of the phrase 'Flippin 'ell!!' as their squads disappeared before their very eyes.

We had now been issued with battledress, boots, a side hat (a glengarry) and short puttees for the War. 'General' was, I learnt, an ex-regular soldier. A wiry

8

little man of quite indeterminate age. His skin was darkened like old leather. Most of us spoke with Westcountry brogue but his accent was indefinable and he spoke in crisp, short, staccato, and often obscene, bursts. He was, even as a gunner, a mine of information about Army theory and practice and one of my erstwhile colleagues reckoned that he had been born - by numbers - on the parade ground of some far-off Colonial Barracks.

My complete innocence and profound ignorance of military matters must have caught his early attention. This War was obviously to be his finest hour and he was already on the promotion ladder. I, in turn, had recognised his supreme craftiness. He was the 'ferret' and I was just about to become one of the helpless rabbits on the stick - if I was not careful.

His first action was to get us 'felled in' and, with his best and loudest military style, he got the six of us marching the few paces across the yard where, as if by magic, he produced a 'brush, individual, soldier, sweeping, for the use of.' With this one brush we only got six sweeps each to clean the Battery Office floor. We then marched - at least he gave the shouted orders - the few paces back towards our kitbags and we 'got felled out'.

Periodically during the rest of the morning the very slow growing squad would be marched to the now opened Quartermasters Store to collect various items of personal equipment that were being unpacked by the Q. Store clerk. 'General' gave a running commentary with explanations on each item.

Early weapons
6 man brush sweeping one

"You've got to sign for each item," he explained, "cos if you buggers lose anything they bastards will charge you for a new one." There was venom in every word. Not against us, for he obviously considered that we in our ignorance were no threat to his superior position.

When we drew two blankets each he explained, "One is for when you is living and the other is for when you is dead. They bastards will wrap you in one before they bury you - and then take a shilling out of your pay."

As light entertainment during waiting we learnt about 'Field Punishments'. How they would tie the victim to the gunwheel during firing and often after rapid fire the crew would have to scrape his remains up and use a blanket for internment before their sergeant indented for another man.

As the morning went by we drew some mess-tins, two ill-fitting metal

9

containers, and while we again sat on our growing kit bags 'General' did one of his star turns. How, during a lull in a battle, 'fatigue parties' went out to tidy up the battle field. How they dug great holes to bury the dead AND the dying and the piles of shit that 'fell out of the buggers'. How the equipment was then

Poor appetites!

tarted up in a cloud of metal polish and blanco before battle recommenced.

At one o'clock twenty of us were marched by 'General' out into the streets of Taunton to a secluded corner of a park where billowing smoke revealed that a tented cookhouse had been set up. On arrival my suspicions were confirmed of the affinity between the Cookhouse and the Sanitary Duties. For that orderly - known affection- ately as the Shit Wallah - had been promoted to chief cook, for his badge of office - crossed drain rods - had been inadvertently left leaning against a boiler.

Our first meal consisted of a brown stew that defied definition, and rice practically unaltered from the raw state. The cook had I figured got the jobs badly mixed up. Two large swill bins at the exit indicated that our appetites were expected to be a little off tune in Wartime.

As was Army custom at each meal, there would be a shout of "Orderly Officer, eyes front!" by the Orderly Sergeant and we would be expected to leap to our feet which could be a bit nasty. Army benches had their legs towards the middle so that the last person seated would collapse to the floor catapulting various items of food and cutlery in all directions. The Officer would quickly chant "Any Complaints? Carry on," and beat a hasty retreat, the Sergeant lingering for a few moments to take the names

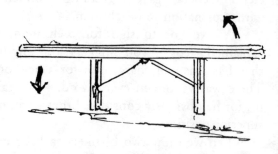

Early weapons - The tip-cat bench

of anyone foolish enough to complain and thus qualify later for his ready-made fatigue party. On exit we dipped our mess-tins in greasy tepid water.

During the afternoon the War made little more progress but we did acquire an Army ground sheet each. This waterproof square was to lay under our two blankets but was also a sort of cape, so designed as to run rain water either straight into the tops of the boots or into the trouser pockets.

At teatime we discovered that the Army had only cocoa and that Army mess-tins containing a hot liquid could painfully burn the lips.

After returning to the Barracks the evening started with the Town boys turning up in force, signing in and fleeing from the scene like scalded cats. But worse was to come for me. My name appeared on a list for billeting after I explained that I had no real relations in Taunton. My first mistake of the War.

Twenty of us gathered up our two blankets and kitbags and General marched us out of the barracks into Taunton's busy streets: a despondent reminder to the inhabitants that the dreaded War had started. We must have looked a sorry sight. A relic, a ghostly return to Taunton of the defeated Yokels from the Battle of Sedgemoor.

My arms began to ache as, marching in the road, we dodged the traffic round corners and up side streets where finally a sergeant was waiting.

"Squad, Sqd ht!!" yelled General which slowly brought us to a stop and started several dogs barking. We dropped our belongings in the road and fished in our pockets to find our hats.

"This place wot you are looking at," said General with obvious great glee, "is your new home."

It looked more like a semi-derelict house. We filed inside; four men to a room. There was no floor covering or furniture of any sort, no lights and the place sounded hollow and was damp and chilly. General was as usual very helpful, explaining that we must get our blankets laid out before dark as no lights were working, we should use our kit bags as a pillow, and that as we were 'On active service' we must not change into civilian clothes.

His final remark was "Make the most of this luxury while it fucking lasts."

It was now 19.00 hrs and we were free. My battledress was ill fitting. My boots were stiff and Taunton's streets were now completely empty; the hob nails echoed round the buildings so that I could not escape my own footsteps. The civilian population had retired behind heavy curtains in apparent deep shock. The cinemas were closed and the pubs almost silent, empty and cheerless.

I must have walked miles into the night. There seemed no glory, no object in my plight. The image of wretched rabbits awaiting certain and uncomplaining death cluttered my mind - the hanging carcasses - the ultimate fate of men and animals alike.

At length I returned to the billet. In one room someone had got a flickering candle casting eerie shadows through the open doors. In my dark room three pinpoints of light indicated that my pals were already in 'bed' - smoking, the fumes temporarily masking the stale smell of dampness.

We all stayed in our underclothes. The boards were hard and unforgiving as the silent hours passed. Only broken by the noises of two comrades in another room, obviously slightly drunk, vainly trying to find the entrance between their blankets.

Before that I had heard the gentle closing of the outside door - that was General going out for the night.

CHAPTER THREE
AT GROUND LEVEL

"It's eating in bed what brings the rats," said General the next morning as some twenty bleary-eyed Gunners assembled in the road to march to Taunton's swimming baths. This was the Army's response when one of our number complained that we had only one cold tap and basin in the billet. At least the cold water would remove the worst of the grime.

General went on the tell us of the time when he once took a Mars Bar to his bed on the floor, and how he battled all night with a great army of furry monsters who apparently lived on a diet of chocolate and human testicles. "The fucking Army don't like men who sing soprano" was his final piece of advice.

Of course none of us had bathing trunks but General said the water was so cold that our manhood would be so shrunk that one would think "we was a flipping lot of girls." We were beyond bothering.

We were then, via the billet, marched dejectedly to breakfast at the cookhouse.

At 09.00hrs we were back at the Barracks to be joined by the local lads for a rollcall. Then having changed into overalls - as we only had one uniform - we did a bit of either marching drill or an exercise pretending to move the two old Howitzers that had got stuck in the mud. This was called 'without drag ropes prepare to advance'. I assumed that drag ropes were in short supply. At sporadic intervals we collected odd bits of equipment from the Q Stores.

The Town lads did not seem to take matters very seriously and the Officers seemed to be mostly conspicuous by their absence. We assumed they were running the War from the comfort of Taunton's County Hotel. There were forays to the Cookhouse for meals but as our reports reached those still living at home, attendance was patchy much to the benefit of local pigs who ate the swill.

If Tauntonians were reminded of the Battle of Sedgemoor then a twice weekly route march could have done nothing to dispel their fears. For this exercise the Battery Captain, a tall willowy man who slightly wobbled when he tried to stand to attention, would march straight out of the Main Gate - clutching his little cane and a crumpled map of Greater Taunton. Ten paces behind -just out of whispering distance - would march the Battery Sergeant Major complete with 'poached egg' on sleeve and boots a-shining. And behind him at the longest distance permissible - in approximately three ranks - all those members of 373 Field Artillery Battery RA TA who could not present an adequate excuse for not taking an afternoon walk. Around these men circled sundry sergeants, like mountain sheep dogs, barking 'Left - Left - Left, Right, Left' and other less military remarks.

Marching in the rear was the ample figure of Sergeant 'Bodger' Howe, whose sole duty was to collect the debris left in the road as the column proceeded.

Early Army battledress was designed in three stock sizes. Gigantic, medium and dwarf. The Q Stores had often to hand out what was available without reference to the shape of the recipient. Add to this the carrying of gasmask, gas cape, full harness - complete with ammunition pouches and water bottle - and the dreaded short puttees. These would quite often slowly unwind during bursts of activity, so that the following soldier treading on the end would cause the victim to fall to the ground like a Mahomedan saying his prayers; but of course using a four-letter Anglo Saxon version of the words. All this would lead to hats and bits of equipment being dislodged. In one extreme case one victim nearly lost his trousers.

These early route marches were a great opportunity for singing. The old War songs of 1914-18 quickly lost favour except 'There's a long long trail a-winding' sung to waltz time and the Volga Boat Song sung at slow speed. Both designed to cause chaos with the pace and would invariably lead to a spell of 'Marching to attention' until the pace rate was again stabilised at some 120 per minute.

Another favourite was the 'Quartermaster's Store':
  'There were rats, rats, big as bloomin' cats,
  In the store. In the store.
  There were rats, rats, big as blooming cats.
  In the Quartermaster's Store.'

CHORUS
'Mine eyes are dimmed, I cannot see,
I have not brought my specs with me,
I have not brought my specs with me.'

The Q Stores would then be credited with having all manner of things both obscene and blasphemous. This often meant another spell of march but not usually before some dear elderly ladies had stopped to look and listen to 'our dear boys', only to scuttle away in confusion when the words became apparent.

The Captain would have great difficulty in preserving his aloofness and dignity when he was leading us up side streets, often lined by mums, girlfriends and sundry children. And all of them intent on disrupting the orderly progress of the column. Some friends claimed that the Captain, in the ensuing confusion, would lead the column past the same place twice.

The final indignity would always come after an hour's trek and the Barracks would be in sight. This is when we all sang the Battery's Battle Song with great gusto:

'We are the lads of the 373,
We cannot fight, we cannot fuck -
No fucking good are we!! ...'

It never had a second verse for a yell would go out from the front for us to 'march to attention'.

On entering the Barrack Square the Officer would disappear towards the Mess - to have a stiff whisky, we guessed - and the Sergeant Major would quickly dismiss the parade so that Sergeant Howe, by now a cross between Father Xmas and a cricket umpire, could distribute lost property.

After a week of discomfort and a degree of indignity I was paraded with all those who had not wangled themselves an administrative job. I was fallen out with a group who had held up their hands declaring that they could drive a car.

"You lot," barked the Sergeant Major, "are now 'drivers IC'

Last man

wot stands for internal combustion because we no longer have horses." Both West and North Somerset Yeomanry were horsed units by tradition. Although it was comforting to know that I would drive a vehicle if we had any, I did not, at that moment, fancy polishing and cleaning the one 30cwt truck that already had a rather possessive driver.

The S.M. then produced a set of signallers by asking if anyone had ever used

15

a telephone. The rest were installed as gunners with the words "and the rest of you used catapults at school."

Faced with the prospect of polishing lorries, reeling out miles of telephone line or moving guns without drag-ropes I decided to do something for myself. During the slow process of listing names I dodged out of line, joined a squad marching across the square and then dived into a small hut I knew was occupied by a little-known Artillery sect called 'Specialists'. Inside, an elderly Officer, of Great War Vintage, was apparently talking about the development of the Artillery Piece from the days of the cannon ball. In the front row sat several junior Officers (known as two-loots) and behind then some ten men also on chairs. I slipped in very low and quietly and sat in the back row in the middle of one of the notorious Army 'tip-up' benches.

When the lecture ended the men all jumped up to let the Officers escape. At this point I realised I was probably the only loose gunner in the Battery without his name on a list, so I chased after one of the more innocuous and frail looking 'two loots' who was carrying some books. I saluted with gusto, almost losing my hat and my puttees, and told him he had not got my name on his list of Specialists. Without hesitation and with a "Jolly good, all right Smith - I'll see to that. Report here every morning at 9 o'clock," he scuttled away, leaving me standing alone. I was just looking for somewhere to bolt for cover when a roar arose from the direction of the Battery Office and the Battery Sergeant Major indicated that my presence was immediately required. He was a pale shade of puce as he glared at me.

"Did I see you approach and speak to an Officer?"

"Yes, Sgt Major, I -"

But I got no further. I had apparently committed a cardinal sin.

"No gunner will EVER go up and speak to an Officer without prior permission from a senior N.C.O. and with a N.C.O. present - see!"

I was already allergic to Sergeant Majors. The feeling was now mutual.

During the next two weeks I found this almost impossible to obey, for the Specialists often had a few Officers at the lectures. When we went out with a tape measure and 'director'(a simple theodolite) into Taunton's Vivary Park to take angles we had an Officer but no N.C.O. with us. I also did a three day course at a school in Exeter where the lectures were about tactics and the

Magic

course at a school in Exeter where the lectures were about tactics and the structure of an Infantry Division. I almost filled a note book and, to my delight, found that if I held it or an odd gunnery form in my hand I was strangely exempt from the attention of the Sergeant Major. It was a sort of military wand. Even General did not question my absence from the marching to and from the billet if I walked off clutching a piece of paper. However I always used General as a military source of all wisdom.

His theory about men speaking to Officers was that the latter were all 'pansies' and that all the gunners, with the possible exception of a few of the Specialists, were all virile men. To allow Officers to mix without being chaperoned would cause trouble. Of course General did not put it quite as delicately as that; but I would be wary of Officers from then on.

Taunton's dark, lengthening evenings were a very strange world for me. The clatter of my hob-nail boots would echo around the empty darkened streets; I could never seem to escape. The pubs were sad and almost deserted as I sat with my depressed colleagues trying to make a half pint of scrumpy cider last all evening.

But a lonely young soldier wandering the dim-lit streets at night was, according to General - at his most descriptive - easy prey for the frightening attentions of what General called 'Hewers'. These voracious females would lure the unwary - 'like moths to a fucking candle' - up the darkened side streets to their flea-ridden dens. There to quickly relieve him of his manly vigour and cast him out panting and forlorn - minus any remnants of cash or valuables - back on to the street... but worse.

'Hewers', according to General, were all 'pox-ridden'. Any young soldier sampling their wares would be 'pissing fucking needles by the morning'. For such cases the Army had special Medical Treatment Centres where the sadistic orderlies of the Medical Corps were trained in the art of bayonet practice.

"Mates," General would say, gathering our attention "You want to see they poor bastards." He would hold up his hand as if in dire despair. "Lined up there, bollock naked - bent right over -

'Hewers'

and there they was, them orderlies, bastard great syringes at the ready."

"At the pres- ent -" (a colleague beside me gasped in pain and disbelief) "Sure!" said General and then the order FIX - and on go the needles - and then CHARGE!!!" He always related the last bit with obvious relish. "You should have seen 'em. Gaaaaawd!! Flippin' Double Top mates. Yell - Shriek they would. Twice every day - when they weern't scrubbing the floors."

General had explained to us that the ordinary soldier is only good if he has what he called 'The Hate.'

After a week I could see what General meant. The official line was one of continual 'punishment'. When after three weeks I learnt via one of the Officers that the Battery was going down near Dartmoor I had at first assumed thet we 'other ranks' were to be given a spell of real Prison Life.

It was a comfortless drizzly autumn day that the men of 373 Battery RA TA marched with their belongings to Taunton Railway Station. For most it meant leaving the comforts of home and there were tearful farewells on the platform. For twenty of us it meant the end - for the time being - of living at ground level.

CHAPTER FOUR

GLORIOUS DEVON...
THE PHONEY WAR

"... and remember the honour and good name of the Battery," said Captain Bridges at the end of his little speech to three very wavy lines of soldiery in the Square at Holesworthy -in deepest, darkest Devon. Then with the inevitable "Carry on Sgt Major," he hastened across the road to the Mess in the sanctuary of the White Hart Hotel.

Sgt Major Starr, with a glint of delight in his eye, then translated the Captain's words concerning private billets; as if the Territorial Volunteers had all been raised in doss-houses, borstals or other penal establishments. He concluded -

"Try to treat yer landlady something like yer mother. No booze in the bedrooms - no pissing on the stairs - and always remember to pull the chain."

Once again I had the terrible feeling of being a rabbit carcass on a stick. In my ignorance I had again slipped up.

We were draped in full harness and carried our half-full kitbags and now had two blankets over our shoulders. Resembling the last remnants of a defeated Napoleonic rabble, we were led off from the Square around the little market Town led by a Sergeant, with a much pencilled map, and Sid - an erstwhile friend from early T.A. days - who had been appointed billeting clerk, carrying his valued piece of paper called a nominal roll.

At about every fifth house the column would stop. Sid would call out a couple of names and the depleted column would close up and continue with decreasing numbers and increasing dejection. My turn came late.

I had arranged to share a billet with Sid who guaranteed us the very best - next door to the Cinema and with an older couple who would have an assortment of younger relations calling in. Sid's kit had been delivered by lorry and all our blankets were soon incorporated into the beds in the best front bedroom. We were accepted as sons and would be offered a constant refuge from the absurdities of Army life. I soon found Sid, who had gained a stripe, to be a mine of information on beating the system.

The Battery H.Q. had established itself in the old T.A. huts down the road past the Parish Church. There being no square outside, we lined up in the road for morning roll call and to take the Salute from an officer. We would then 'march' away in various groups - drivers, signallers, the sick and finally the Specialists. None of the 'staff' - such as cooks, orderlies, batmen, office and store people - were ever seen on a parade. They were in my view the 'ferrets'.

There were in Taunton some twenty Specialists, but I soon discovered that most of these had applied to be Officers. Two had, I knew, joined the Battery as 'two loots', many more had gone to Officer training and the rest had either gone on leave, become 'staff' or just not turned up.

And so after a week I was the only Specialist on the rollcall and had tacked on the end of the signallers to escape from the parade. I was making my way back to the Billet, to perhaps have a lie down and decide my next move, and was creeping past the White Hart but my footsteps must have betrayed me.

"I say - Smith." A loud call came from one of the windows. I stifled a cry of "Oh, bugger," for I realised this was one of our ex-specialist 'two loots' - affectionately known as 'Lt Pullthrough', who may have known a little too much about my habits.

"Sir!" I replied with a faked enthusiasm, as I wheeled around to see what countenance he wore and if the Sgt. Major was to witness me talking to an Officer through the window of the Mess - probably a capital offence.

"I say - Smith. I'm sorry we can't give you any specialist training. Go to the Battery Office and draw the 'Manual of Artillery Survey'. Read that - tell them I said so!"

It was thus not long before I was once again stealthily creeping back to my billet with the Manual, the largest piece of paper the Battery provided.

"Are you there Sid?"

20

Next morning I planned to take the Manual on Parade and hold it at the 'low trail' during the inspection to perhaps taunt the Sgt Major. However 'Pullthrough' sent for me early and - I thought rashly, as my only known skill was rabbit catching - commanded that I assist the Ration Clerk on Mondays and the medical orderly on Tuesdays. On Thursdays I was to help Sid to pay out the Landladies in the labour exchange (using the Army Green form marked horses/men), and on Fridays I was to assist one Officer as he paid the men at pay parade.

Clutching a handful of assorted papers and the Manual I went to the Q. Stores where, behind a scribbled notice 'AIN'T GOT NONE', and concealed behind a mountain of spare blankets and almost empty shelves, I found Sid with his feet up reading a book. He seemed pleased with his protégé.

My duties were neither arduous nor difficult, about an hour each day, but it did allow me to study in depth the ways of becoming a permanent 'ferret', of getting maximum leave and (although it took me nearly three years) of getting my name removed from the pays-sheets without losing pay. My early discovery was that all duties were taken from the pay sheets.

I didn't need to attend parades any more, and as Sid undertook not to issue the Battery Office with an extra chair I volunteered to find my own desk elsewhere in the Town. Usually an armchair by the fire, a cafe, the Library or even in bed.

After three weeks I heard, on my short daily voyage of discovery to the Office, that Pullthrough had been commanded to find some Specialists.

Lt. Pullthrough - so called by the lads because, in military terms, he did resemble the piece of 4x2 cloth used to clean the inside of a rifle barrel - was a man of action. He was said to have fallen over once on parade whilst trying to 'about turn'. I suspected that this would be an added reason why the Sgt Major would not want men to approach him directly in case his trouble was contagious.

Lt Pullthrough found a disused schoolroom in the town; the Regiment also provided a hundredweight of assorted gunnery pamphlets, pro-formas, and survey tables. He produced a director (a theodolite), a large artillery range-finder, plane tables, rulers, chinagraph pencils, a slide rule, a tape measure, wooden battens, hessian, loofahs, and a pile of empty matchboxes. He also had found three other Specialists and one of these had the two stripes of a Bombardier. His intention was for us, in the real absence of weaponry, to go to War on a pencil and pro-forma.

Reg, our Bombardier, was, I knew, an extremely crafty operator. He was an ex-bank clerk, recently married in Taunton and specialised in getting long weekend leave. My other colleagues were Harry, an infant school teacher who was far removed from the warrior class. Then there was Jim who actually was a surveyor with the Somerset County Council. As I explained to them, if we ever got stranded in the countryside I could always catch them a rabbit dinner.

Our first task was to build a miniature range: a foot-to-the-mile replica of an area of pretend Devon, made of hessian stretched on a wooden frame. Houses were made of matchboxes, hedges of loofahs, rivers, ponds, streams and roads were strips of paper. Once all glued together and painted it was very pretty. Underneath was a grid angled as if from an imaginary gun sited five miles back. We could now play the game of gunnery by one of us giving firing orders as if at an observation post and another, lying on his back on the floor underneath, sticking a pencil up through to mark the shell burst positions. It was great fun and sometimes our junior Officers would join in. We always allowed them to cheat a bit, as they had not the practice we had and frustration could make them bad tempered.

We also had other games. We had coloured and numbered match boxes to represent every gun and vehicle we should have had in a complete 12 gun mobile Battery. With the aid of the Manuals we learnt to do all the manoeuvring for a leapfrog advance or retreat across the schoolroom floor.

On fine days we would do survey around the Town, traversing or intersecting with our equipment, being careful to arrive outside pubs, cafes, the Dugout (the Holesworthy Ladies Welfare Canteen) or our billets for frequent breaks.

If ever the Sgt Major planned anything nasty, like an inspection or route march, Reg could be relied upon to get a vehicle and we would motor to Dartmoor to survey around Yes Tor. Only returning when the danger had passed.

Sometimes a few officers would insist on joining in and we would have to wear tin hats and equipment and go to Affland Moor.

The day arrived when a notice was posted up to announce a 'Battery Exercise'. We had only half the necessary men, practically no vehicles, no gun tractors, no ammunition (thank goodness) and a general lack of equipment. It was to be 'unmounted and unarmed', and we thought unimaginable. It was to take place on the Town Football field.

After a great deal of shouting, arm-waving and weaving around, four gun crews were lined up behind their supposed guntractor drivers, likewise command vehicle personnel were lined up behind their driver and the signal trucks. Only one Officer - our lanky Battery Captain Bridges - turned up. We four specialists were behind a supposed driver-i-c and so were excluded from actively shaping events.

The brave Captain was, we noted, armed with a megaphone and a revolver. He was we presumed supposed to represent the O.P. Officer. He asked us all to pretend this was a real action.

Without hesitation but with a certain amount of trepidation in his voice he shouted:

"The Battery will advance!!"

Our experiences had only been with matchboxes. We instantly gathered that the other sections had not had this advantage and that a state of realism was taking over. Some drivers were playing chuff-chuffs. Others were changing pretend spark plugs or changing imaginary wheels. A shout of 'Indians!' went up from the signals 'truck'. Some of the gunners, feigning death from arrows, collapsed on the grass. There were cries of 'Bang, Bang, Bang!' The Battery Captain set off in front of this mob across the field vainly shouting something in his megaphone. It was rather like the first Pantomime of the season.

"Battery ready to move off Sir."

In a short while the men had arrived at the row of garden fences along the far end of the field. The excitement was such that some men were prepared to advance into the gardens and beyond. Anxious civilian faces peered out from the bedroom windows. Our leader was pinned against a post and rail fence - the signals 'truck' next to us said no one knew how to retreat. I had assumed the worst.

But in the obvious great traditions of the British Army our Captain climbed upon a high fence post. With arm outstretched he bellowed "Halt!" with all his might:

"The Battery will ADVANCE - BACKWARDS!"

The day was saved and in the resulting chaos he was last seen scuttling back to the Mess. The Sgt Major assumed command and 'felled' everyone in for a spell of marching drill. Except for the Specialists - Reg managed to smuggle us back to our match boxes via the ladies canteen, the Dugout.

CHAPTER FIVE

THE PHONEY WAR

The Battery exercise in broad daylight had not proved very reassuring for the local populace, although several had assumed it was a military form of rugger. The solution that our seniors produced was both ingenious and simple: NIGHT MARCHES. Once a week, if the weather was fine, the 'rabbits' would parade in the road wearing overalls (strictly no kit), and with a man both front and rear carrying a hurricane lantern the column would proceed along the high banked country lanes around Holesworthy. We specialists - despite Reg's best efforts - joined in. I rather enjoyed the freedom of marching styles it provided. It was more agricultural than military.

There was to be strictly no singing - nor shouting. Just a sort of quiet cursing, some whispering and occasional subdued cries of 'Whur be us to?' in local dialect. The rural area of mid-northwest Devon was good sheep country and, with only a few weeks' practice, the marching lads could give a perfect imitation of an

"Tis them bloody zoldiers again"

escaping flock of sheep. With individual marchers doing the odd 'baa', 'brrr', 'baaaa', 'ba-ba', it was nigh impossible to control the noise and many of the N.C.O.s joined in to break the near silence of the night. Great would be our joy if, after a time, other lanterns and dogs would appear from the fields peering down on the moving column. Often the cry would then pierce the night;

"'Tis them bloody zoldiers agin, you!"

As the very cold winter of 1939/40 approached, the Battery had fully settled in and for me life was very pleasant. Each day, surrounded by our matchbox toys, we specialists would consider ways of making life even more pleasant. Sid, my billet mate, would advise me of impending official activity and I could usually find General lurking around the cookhouse - as Fatigues Bombardier - who would answer my queries on military matters.

Then quite suddenly in late December the whole tone of life was shattered - we were joined by one hundred men of the First Militia. They were, to us, all 'voreigners', all young and from big cities. The accents suggested Glasgow, Liverpool, London and Birmingham. They had learned to hate the Army so, as if to confirm this feeling, the Battery promoted a few new Sergeants to give them a further three weeks of physical training and drill. Discipline was generally tightened. There were to be our own Battery curfew patrols and even the Officers had been motivated to operate outside their Mess in the White Hart. Pullthrough and other two loots would often take refuge in our Command Post - we found it very disturbing. We felt that the less known about our 'training' the better.

Despite my best efforts I would occasionally just slip up and experience the horrible rigours of being an Army 'rabbit'.

After one of my frequent 'leaves' back on the farm I let out to an Officer that I had been shooting rabbits with my shot-gun as they were bolted by ferrets. Next morning my name was on Battery Orders for rifle shooting. Reg insisted that I had volunteered.

I reported in full kit - tin hat, harness, puttees, water-bottle, overcoat, gasmask, gas cape - the lot, having also drawn a rifle from Sid in the stores and rations from the cookhouse. Our party consisted of a bombardier and four men.

After a long journey by lorry we arrived at the ranges. Two hours elapsed before we were marched to the firing position. The place was bristling with Safety Officers, Safety Sergeants, red flags and people with arm bands. The detailed safety procedure was explained to us and, once we were lying flat in the prone position, we were handed five rounds of ammunition each. This was the first occasion in the War that I had seen both ammunition and weapons with the same person. I thought the Army must be getting vicious - someone might get killed!

With all the safety drill it took me ten minutes to fire five rounds. A bren gun was then substituted and we were allowed one burst each. Then we were marched away to watch others from a very safe distance. By this time my water-bottle was in the middle of my stomach, my gas cape was getting loose and I feared a puttee was becoming unravelled. When I jokingly pointed out to a colleague that we didn't shoot a single rabbit he despairingly remarked "Wasted a whole fucking day and didn't shoot one o' they bloody safety bastards either!"

To be ill in the Army was to be defenceless and very plainly was not encouraged. The ferrets contrived to become ill on leave so that their return was delayed by the signature of their local doctor. They could be comfortably ill at home. I however, developed a fever and was covered in a rash while on a trip to Affland Moor and was ordered by an Officer to report sick in the morning. I had tripped up again.

The sick, the lame and the lazy reported to the Orderly Sergeant of the day outside the Battery Office at 08.45 each morning. We were then marched half a mile to a cold empty room used for medical inspections. Here we could wait anything up to three hours exchanging experiences, infections or just groaning. On the arrival of the Medical Officer and his orderly we were lined up in a draughty passageway to be called in singly to receive diagnosis and sentence.

For minor ills the Army had two cures. The No 9 laxative pill that was said to even bolt the rats from the sewers, and Army 'Mystic Spec' that was said to taste like a mixture of gunpowder and soft soap. Both to be followed up by several days 'light duties' which meant reporting to the cookhouse and doing all the heavy work of scrubbing and dixie bashing under the watchful eye of General. They would then return as wiser and 'fitter' men dedicated in future to suffer minor ailments in silence.

The Medical Officer (one rumour was that he was a partly trained Vet) was assisted by an orderly who acted as liaison between the victim and the Officer who never needed to speak directly to one another; in the best Army traditions.

When my turn came I was stripped to the waist, shivering and covered in a rash. The M.O. murmured something about Rubella and said to the orderly "Get him to hospital."

The lorry that carted me off seemed to do a circular tour of Dartmoor to collect two other victims, and finally arrived at a small institution-like building that the driver said was 'the loony bin'. We dismounted and were taken on a slow tour of the rooms by an irate and distracted orderly who said they were full up and so he would have to turn someone out.

After some very foul language and a lot of shouting a bed was found and I was thrown three blankets: "One extra for the dying," General had told me. Still wearing my underclothes I struggled between the blankets and awaiting my fate.

There was another bed alongside mine and I was not clear whether the occupant was hiding, asleep or even perhaps dead. It was sometime later and I was beginning to unfreeze when the corpse peered out from his blankets.

"What you in for, mate?" His voice sounded as if he had swallowed a nutmeg grater.

"Measles - I think," I replied in a wavering voice.

"Bloody hell, mate!" he croaked, "I've been in this dump for a month now - came in with a bad arm - the bastard Typhoid jab -caught the lot I have."

"How's that?" I innocently asked. But this only served to bring my companion to deeper despair.

"Once you get in this dump, mate, they shift you around until you catch everything." He was reduced to short spluttering wheezy sentences. "And now I'm to get bloody measles - am I?"

"Sorry," I mumbled when he had settled down a bit. And then a terrible thought occurred to me. "What had the bloke got that was in this bed then? The one they just turned out for me?"

"Him - that poor bastard - I reckon he had Bubonic Plague or something - he was too ill to argue - that's why they turned him out." He fell back in silence.

I pictured this poor sod now in the cookhouse doling our the butter and opening the tins of jam after collapsing when cleaning dixies or shifting the coal.

The next day I was moved to a larger room where I quickly learnt about the working of the embryo Army Medical Services. The 'Hospital' was run by one RAMC Corporal assisted, or hindered, by one private they appropriately called 'Blackie'. It was in a spare wing of a Mental Hospital and I was reassured to learn that the elderly, mumbling, swaying and arm-waving men that were often visible through the windows were not indeed our own young men after treatment.

Blackie seemed to spend all day unsuccessfully battling with the boiler which justly earned him his nickname and led to cold rooms and equally cold food - delivered by lorry from some distant cookhouse. Blackie dished it out and supplied his own description of the cuisine:

"Fucking swill - and bloody cold as well!"

The stay in 'hospital' was governed mainly by the state of the 'temperature and pulse' chart at the bottom of each bed. Anyone being discharged on a Friday could ask for weekend leave and see their own home doctor. The Corporal used to hand around thermometers in the morning just after a tepid cup of Army cocoa was put by each bed. By judiciously dipping the thermometer in both mouth and cocoa it was possible to reach the magic 98.4

28

on the Friday - or anything up to about 102 on any other day. The pulse could be increased by having just run up and down the stairs. It had become a sort of Wartime skill. My hospital stay was thus crowned by a week at home starting with a voice like a nutmeg grater.

I had suspected that one of the most boring and useless jobs in the Army was guard duty. Especially so when there was nothing much worth guarding or, for that matter, to guard it with. It was the one activity that, from my observation, the Army could excel in its stupidity. So I had used any ruse, from just going on leave to semi-bogus clerical duties or courses, to avoid doing a 24 hour guard duty.

It was a cold night in February when I slipped up. My name appeared for duty for next day on the evening Battery Orders outside the Office. I was given the next afternoon off to clean and Blanco my harness, polish my boots, press my trousers, shine my badges and generally tidy up under the general heading of Bullshit. I would also draw a rifle to polish.

The Guard consisted of six men, a bombardier and a sergeant. We paraded in the road and after numerous inspections - culminating with the Orderly Officer's - we were marched to the football field where our two highly polished guns were positioned towards a far hedge.

From what I had seen of the Army so far, Guard Duties seemed to be the most mis-directed, inefficient and futile way of protecting Army property. To have a sentry, kit highly polished and gleaming, standing exposed and unarmed - with just a pickaxe handle or a rifle without bullets - could also be, in Wartime, even suicidal. Our Battery guard at Holesworthy had two men stationed at the gates at either end of the football field. Our two highly polished 18 pounder Howitzers were positioned - like farm machinery - along one distant hedge. A couple of properly trained enemy soldiers could, I thought, easily demolish the Battery Office, stores and spike the two guns even

before knifing the two sentries and setting fire to the guardhouse.

When after many months my name appeared on the Guard list I knew I would be sampling a new and frustrating experience: a negation of everything I had learnt in farming, stalking, and as a rabbit catcher.

I left the protection of the Command Post and had the afternoon free to Blanco my harness and gas-mask case, polish my boots

29

and a rifle and dress up in full kit. This was so restricting that only formal movements were possible. At 18.00 hrs I was lined up with five other unfortunates, a bombardier and a Gun Sergeant for numerous adjustments of kit and inspections and finally peered at - in the growing gloom - by the Orderly Officer - a 'two-loot' who appeared as bored with the whole proceedings as we were.

With the usual shouted commands we were then marched to our base for the next twenty-four hours. This was a converted hen-house with a coal burning stove which I quickly learnt smoked so badly that the door had to be left wide open. It was in fact only lit for a few minutes in a vain attempt to heat the cold food delivered from the cookhouse or warm the cocoa bucket - which was heavily tainted with soot - both in and out. We guards were to do two hours on sentry duty and fours hours off, resting on two blankets on the bare boards.

At ten o'clock that night, thoroughly grimed by the smoke, I was marched out to relieve the man on the far gate for my two hour spell. It was a cold dry night with a thin breeze moving the billowing clouds quickly across the sky so that the moon could peep out to glint on the shining dew or polished metal - a good night for snaring rabbits.

I leaned on the gate for a while listened to the noises across in the Town slowly dying down - little flecks of light in upper windows indicating that the citizens were off to bed. Across the field I could hear the other sentry pacing up and down on the concrete pad at the opposite gate.

I, by instinct, only walked on soft grass and lurked in the shadows of the hedges.

Presently I heard the weird cry of a vixen out across the fields. A faintly squeaking shrew rustled among the leaves of the ditch and then the double thump of a suspicious rabbit sounded along the hedge. When a tawny owl started clicking its beak in the oak above me I knew that I could use Nature's guards to keep watch for me.

Time went by very slowly and by eleven o'clock a few spots of light rain darkened the sky so I emerged from the shadows to look at the two guns, the object of our duty - or so I thought. I listened to the tap - tap - tap of the other sentry at the top gate.

Suddenly I heard other faint footsteps and a challenge followed by the entire Guard turning out for an Officer's inspection. When the commotion stopped I heard footsteps coming across the field. I stealthily crept towards the figure so that I was between him and our guns.

"Halt - who goes there?" I bellowed in my sharpest voice, shining my torch directly in his face, a trick I learnt in dealing with poachers back at home.

30

"Commanding Officer."

"Advance friend and be recognised."

What he said next coloured my entire service from then on.

"Why have you deserted your post?" he barked; but he never gave me time to reply. "Do you realise you could be court marshalled for deserting you post?" he bellowed. "Get back to the concrete pad at your gate."

He turned on his heel and went back from whence he came.

I found I was very angry as I got to the concrete. It was perhaps lucky that he thought that arguing with a mere gunner was totally beneath his dignity. He was not only a Major but a Solicitor, I believed.

I was now to mindlessly pace the concrete. My only enemy was not perhaps Hitler but our own Officers - as General had once explained to us, "A good soldier learns to hate."

In the darkness of the night I felt like a caged animal. As I paced I thought of ways of at least uncaging my mind. My torch could not be used to read a book even if I had one. I searched into my greatcoat pocket and brought out a copy of Reader's Digest. It fell open at a poem - about War. I had hated poetry at school but at this moment I hated something else even more. I pulled out the page and stuck it deep in the foliage of the bank. I would march up and down that pad and each time I reached that end I would use my torch to learn a new line. So it was that at the end of my two dark sentry duties I learnt that poem:

> You that have faith to look with fearless eyes
> Beyond the tragedy of a world of strife
> And trust that out of night and death shall rise
> The dawn of ampler life.
>
> Rejoice whatever anguish rend your heart
> That God has given you for a priceless dower
> To live in these great times and play your part
> In freedom's crowning hour.
>
> That you may tell your sons who see the light
> High in the heavens their heritage to take.
> I saw the powers of darkness put to flight;
> I saw the morning break.

When I got back to the hut I found myself still mumbling the last line - and

I found I had shed one puttee on my beat. I was no longer angry.

During the next day we received two Battery prisoners and I had to do a spell between sentry duty of watching them perform 'modern' punishments. The Guard Sergeant said I was forbidden to give them a hand or even chat with them so I could only talk to them in whispers.

One was digging a two-foot cubic hole in the hard ground with a small spade in full kit. As soon as he was finished, the Orderly Officer would be called to throw an initialled cigarette packet in the bottom of the hole. The unfortunate was then made to fill the hole in. The Officer would then ask for the packet - with his initials on it - so he would have to dig it out again. This was repeated. As a break from this the prisoner, again in full kit, had four dummy marked shells weighing about 25 lbs each. Two were placed at opposite ends of the football field. The unfortunate man had to change them over every half hour; which meant continually running across the field with a shell under his arm.

As I was sure General would have said, "If the guns had been firing they could have been tied to the gun wheel." So they were perhaps lucky.

The next day I resumed my gentle specialist activities, no longer wondering why so many of our number had applied for Officer training. Being an Army 'rabbit' could be very humiliating.

As the first winter of the War was coming to an end, the Battery was said to have its full complement of men. It was divided into Battery H.Q. and three Troops A, B and C. We gained three new specialists from the Militia, and Reg was made a sergeant - mainly to ensure that we were not taken off for other duties without the permission of Pullthrough.

There were two jobs we often volunteered for. The Battery coal wagon would arrive at Holesworthy Station every two weeks at about Friday mid-day, the normal fatigue party unloading it into sacks on Saturday morning. Any four of us wishing extended weekend leave could, stripped to the waist, unload this, have a bath and get the early evening train to home on the Friday.

The other duty was the Curfew Patrol - two gunners and a bombardier - who walked all the streets for an hour after 10.30 wearing arm-bands. The fun here was that several of the local young ladies had been trained to undress behind thin curtains looking on to the streets. A minor peep show; the patrol not being responsible for the blackouts.

The greatest item of new equipment was the replacement canvas puttee. But we still only had the two old guns, about twelve rifles and one Bren gun. The Army had given us several khaki-painted old motorcars: this enabled the

Battery to do one small convoy exercise. I also got special permission to take a car from the 'Wagon Lines' each Sunday to take a load of believers to the R.C. Churches at either Bude - on fine days - or Launceston on dismal days. Thus I avoided the great Sunday Church parade to the Parish Church.

The vehicle parks were always called 'Wagon Lines' in the Yeomanry because, one always felt, they had mourned the passing of the horse. Further, General maintained that drivers i.c. still had the right to urinate against the offside wheel and small wet puddles along a road would indicate the a Yeomanry convoy had passed that way.

Officers will be mounted

Our Officers had got a pack of foxhounds - who used to live well off the swill from the Cookhouse. They borrowed a motley group of horses for fox-hunting. Other ranks could proceed on foot if they promised to shout 'Tally-Ho!' and not 'There the fucking bugger goes!' on seeing the fox.

The tranquillity of Army life - especially for the 'ferrets' - had led me to think that it would be a pity to ever move until the War was over. But Sid had, in late

"They're moving"

April, been alerted to spend a day in Tavistock with an Officer looking out new billets - and especially a good one near the cinema for ourselves. When I consulted General he assured me that an Army unit could not stay more that nine months in one place because, as he so delicately put it, "you fucking bastards would cause so many little problems." From observations of many of the local maidens he could be exactly right.

In early May even the Officers came out in force to join in the pretend 'battles' of Affland Moor with pretend guns and pretend vehicles. It was a cross between botany and elementary survey. Unfortunately on Friday 10th May our real enemy, the Hun, had also been doing some exercises which resulted in the invasion of Holland and Belgium.

On that day the men were confined to the Battery Office area. I however was detailed to spend the day in the Holesworthy Labour Exchange paying out our gallant landladies for the last time - a job which my colleagues described as 'the catastrophe clerk'. I also learnt that we'd changed our Commanding Officer.

The new chief was a fiery little man, much loved by many local volunteers.

He was reputed to be a no-nonsense Exmoor farmer affectionately known as Oscar.

After dark that night we all collected our kit and paraded at the Holesworthy Railway Station. The good citizens of Holesworthy turned out in force to bit farewell and I saw some were in tears. The night was hot and we waited some time on the platform with the engine snorting disapproval, the wisps of steam catching the light from the flickering torches of the officers and senior ranks.

When they started fitting eight men into a compartment I decided to break ranks and wander around with the remaining parts of some billeting payment sheets I had that day failed to hand in at the Battery Office. I discovered, to my delight, that they were already searching out for me to share a whole compartment with the Bombardier in charge of the Bren gun. This was the last compartment before the guns which were on flat-bottom trucks. We even had two boxes of ammunition. Further, that he had orders to open fire if the train was attacked.

We put the loaded Bren on the floor with two full boxes of ammunition. We had just settled along the seats on either side when the train gave a lurch forwards and we started moving out into the starry night - going east.

CHAPTER SIX

THE TIME OF DUNKIRK

This was not a corridor train so, as we sped along the darkened countryside and through occasional stations during the night, we had little contact with anyone else. There were a couple of stops outside stations when it appeared that the engine was taking on water and the Battery members were taking the opportunity to let off 'water'.

Bombardier Sykes had, I knew, been a regular soldier and seemed to relish almost single-handedly defending the Battery. He must have wondered, as I did, why a mere specialist had been entrusted with refilling his magazines should he need to fire at the enemy. He did not like my idea of trying a pot-shot at some rabbits along the embankments.

After several hours we stopped in a darkened station and peering out of the window we could hear someone shouting "Everyone out! Fall in on the platform." As we gathered our kit and got the Bren and ammunition boxes out there were the inevitable muted witty cries of "All change" and "Mind the doors". We set up our Bren again in the near darkness and watched the assembled lines of men gathered further along the platform.

I did a small reconnaissance before we got any definite orders; my theory being that a soldier cannot disobey orders until he gets some. This was East Grinstead Station and there were lorries waiting outside. Although Bombardier Sykes climbed aboard a lorry with the Bren, I was directed to the end of a column of men waiting to march away down the road.

With a lantern fore and aft this was like the night marches back in Devon. Now we were all silent. We had no weapons and no real training as infantry.

35

I'm sure most of us were a little frightened - at least no one was brave enough to start up the prophetic old 373 Battery Marching Song -

"We cannot fight - no fucking good are we."

After what seemed about five miles the column turned off the metalled road, through some iron gates, and there on the lawn of an obviously disused country Mansion was our pile of kitbags. Having emerged from a giant rugger scrum and dumped my kitbag in a room marked Battery H.Q., I quickly slid out of the door to look around in the first grey lights of dawn.

The place was called 'Impens' and I saw the largest golden carp that I had ever seen in the pond across the lawn. Dense woodland surrounded the extensive garden and what looked like badger or deer tracks made off into the undergrowth - a good place to hide.

I was making my way back to the room when I dropped my guard to watch a spotted flycatcher nesting in the creeper and just in time to meet Lt Pullthrough.

"Aah, Smith, have you got anything to do yet?" Perhaps he thought I was looking out for some rabbits to snare. "Come with me." He led me back out to the lawn where a lorry was unloading about fifty rifles and several boxes of ammunition.

"Get the numbers and a signature for any you let out." He handed me a small notebook and a pencil. I sat on a box trying to record the individual numbers stamped on each rifle.

Barely a minute had passed before a sergeant and a group of the lads came rushing up demanding twenty rifles and ammunition. I,

Three left

as a mere gunner just told him to help himself, for when I hesitated he shouted at me: "Bloody parachutists have landed, men - quick!"

He disappeared with his men into the woods. No sooner had he gone when another sergeant repeated the whole procedure. As I watched them almost clear my stock I suggested that their chief danger was being shot by the group already in the woods although with our training so far they would be unlikely to hit anything.

Trade was so brisk that by the time Pullthough returned I only had one rifle left with a signature and I had issued that to myself.

Pullthrough was just beginning to chew me up for disobedience of orders when a L.D.V. (Home Guard) man appeared at the gate on his bicycle to say that what the old lady in the local village of Forest Row really saw was a small flock of seagulls. Then the two lots of rifles came back.

Pullthrough told me that our Major had ordered that all personnel must keep under cover in case of air attack. He managed to get the best front room in Impens - it had a lock on the door and an ostrich egg decorating the light cable in the ceiling. I was to use the front bow window as a counter. Soon all the rifles were returned and I had also inherited the Bren and ammunition boxes. The Battery Captain then brought a large pack of cigarettes and I was ordered to sell

The Shop

these at a cut rate when I could spare time from booking rifles. In ten minutes I was appealing for more.

By Whit Monday, 13th May 1940, only two days later, I had a pile of sheets of paper detailing the adventures of the rifles. The shop was now stocked with cigarettes, sweets, chocolates, fruit and a few newspapers. I also had a wireless and with stunned silence a few of us would listen to the news. I rarely left the shop.

By this time all the Battery 'Rabbits' were doing patrol sentry duty, and so I had to open the shop at any time a few faces appeared at the window in daylight. I ate my meals in the shop and slept on a straw palliasse on the ammunition boxes with the loaded Bren pointing out of the window after dark.

The Orderly Officer of the day would pay me a visit to collect the cash and take an order for further requirements. I would sometimes go to East Grinstead with the Battery Clerk to get new supplies. When I started selling beer I met my first real trouble.

I had a box of oranges that were unsaleable and so just gave them away. That evening a few of the lads became a little excitable after too much beer and a battle of rotten oranges ensued. There was a meeting in the shop that night when Oscar was there with Pullthrough and the Sergeant Major.

The result was that I lost the rifles to the Q. Stores - I gathered that my friend Sid should have been doing it all the time. I was now to do daily stock taking, never open after 18.00 hrs or more than two hours at a stretch, never give credit - and NOT to again put the Battery Captain's name on the slate with the other names by the window when I let him have his morning paper one day without paying. Further, a N.C.O. and one man would call each morning to tidy the place up. Finally I should try to get out each afternoon for a couple of hours.

It was not many days before remnants of the British Army were coming back across the Channel (The Dunkirk Harriers), and often very late at night a few bedraggled and demoralised men - still wearing the 45th Divisional symbol (Drakes Drum) would rest for a few hours. I would be roused to open shop and sell them cigarettes and sweets - and hear a few sad stories. One tale was of the Unit who, before surrendering to the Germans, were made to Blanco their kit. The result was that they were accused of using poison gas and were all bayoneted.

Pullthrough then fixed my afternoon break by volunteering me for a special course on the Bren Gun. Occasionally the Army Units would import a few Regular N.C.O.s to stiffen up skills and morale. Bombardier Grimes was a great gangling hulk of a man with a lantern jaw protruding from a face tanned by some tropical sun and chiselled by several long scars that should have been won in noble battle. One scar reached to one side of his lower lip so that his words, in a 'far flung British Empire accent' seemed to tumble out of his face giving him a perpetual grin. His hat was stuck on his head by short hedgehog bristles. I often wondered if Pullthrough had given him a bit of advice about my unmilitary attitude for he always called me 'Squire'. He had no time for Army bullshit.

He took the six of us to the depths of Ashdown Forest for our instruction. At the start of the Course he asked me to demonstrate how, if I was walking along a woodland path, I would react to sighting the enemy.

He bellowed "Enemy one hundred right."

I started to 'become prone' and fumble for the safety catch. I looked around to see what his reactions were but I could see he had fallen backwards off the branch on which he was sitting and was already mumbling helplessly about his 'sainted aunt'. He reckoned that we would have all been shot by the enemy long before I even got the Bren in position.

He then demonstrated how the gun could be brought into action in mid-air as he leapt for cover beside the track in split seconds. Likewise he demonstrated 'air attack', using the Bren light machine gun against aircraft. He trained us all to handle the Bren even wearing blindfolds.

Like General, Bombardier Grimes was a mine of Army stories of valour coupled with absurdity.

When the course finished we all volunteered for his physical training scheme - he would lead a cross country run to view bomb craters and other local sights. We would need to wear only vests, shorts and plimsolls. Our first visit was to a land-mine crater in woodland some two miles distant. We all collected trophies of bits of the green parachute. I was allowed to nominate a volunteer relief man to help in the shop. Life for me was again quite pleasant - I was never given time to worry.

By June 4th 1940 the last of the Dunkirk Harriers had moved inland losing nearly all their weapons - certainly all their guns. It was widely rumoured that Jerry would attack Britain within days.

Our two 18 pounder Howitzers with gun crews left for the coast to fire over open sights. The rest of us then moved just north of Romney Marsh outside the village of Aldington.

The Officers lived in a big house with the stores and offices downstairs. The men lived in bell tents in a dense wood, and I, my Bren gun and a remnant of the shop, lived in the garage.

The next day a load of home-made pikes - sharpened water pipes - and dozens of picks and shovels arrived. Every man had some form of arms and everyone not on patrol guard was to dig concealed trenches - everyone, according to Oscar, meant all Officers as well.

For trench digging we worked in pairs - alternating between pickaxing and shovelling. It was at this that I met one of the strangest and, to me, most delightful characters of the War. His job was a line-signaller, but in peacetime he was a grave digger who spent much time 'shortening' the corpses to economise on coffin size in a large Liverpool Mortuary, so he graphically told me as we worked.

I had spent many hours on the farm digging ditches and clearing roadsides; all rabbit catchers often had to dig out the burrows to retrieve blocked ferrets and rabbits. We reckoned we were the best team in the Battery - at least we knew how to find the easiest digging.

Bono

My mate answered to the name of Bono. He seemed to me prematurely old - he always said he had one foot in the grave. In dim light his deep sunken eyes, round head, short bristly hair and tiny features resembled a walking skull. He was able to stay absolutely still in nearly all positions so that I often thought I was working with a corpse. He often reminded me that, while some people look like their pets, others resemble their jobs - he said I faintly resembled a ferret.

But if his body was still, his mind lived in an exciting fantasy world where even I found it difficult at times to sort fact from fiction.

Our trench was under bushes at the soft sandy corner of a coppice. I reckoned this plot had - very many decades ago - been used as a pets' graveyard. But my colleague swore that these remains were shrunken human bones and that they revealed a litany of murder, suicide and death. Other men would come along to see the remains laid out along our trench - a sort of tourist attraction. He would act as guide.

Bono's most alarming story was that, as the Germans were expected to arrive and shoot us all, Oscar, our chief, had asked him to get the graves dug. They would spare him when he told them his real job. We were in fact digging our own graves and he, Bono, would have to measure every man to ensure that we did enough digging.

We used to get red and yellow alerts that enemy planes had crossed the coast and we reckoned we could hear them in the distance as we were in the trenches. Bono would at these times of stress often go along the trenches and suggest that we should lie flat out and not huddle up as we would be easier for him to 'lay out' if any of us were killed.

His lunacy was carried on at night after I had returned to my garage. Bono used to go around the tents with a tape measure -'getting measurements', as he would say.

So far the Battery had experienced one suicide and two nervous breakdowns and Bono managed to 'measure' one very agitated fellow in his tent late one night. The result was that a screaming lunatic had to be carted off in the night - never to be seen again.

Bombs and land mines could be heard going off around most nights and after dark I would have to take my Bren to a special gun pit in a field overlooking the main wood. There Bombardier Sykes would join me with a box of ammunition and the tripod. We could have then fired on enemy aircraft. In about a week the trenches were dug and there was a 'stand-to' period of one hour at dusk and dawn when every-one would man the trenches and I would go to the Bren gun pit.

Every night enemy aircraft were coming in from the coast and 'red alerts' would be sounded, for the manning of action stations, by the Battery bugler. I had no electric lights in my shop and was not issued with a torch. Everyone, except the Officers and office staff, had to learn to dress and get on station in the varying degrees of total darkness.

After a stand-to at 02.00 one fine night, I was returning with the Bren across the field when I saw a strange glow on a hedge bank. I carefully stalked the light and was amazed to see thousands of tiny lights - they were glow-worms. Collecting a few in a match box I put them on match sticks stuck in the wall above my 'bed' on the floor. After a few minutes they started glowing again and remaining lit up until dawn.

I found that about six acted as a night light and that with three held close to the page on match sticks I could read my local home newspaper - The Chard and Ilminster News.

With the almost constant presence of enemy aircraft apparently patrolling the coastal areas all lights were forbidden in the tented camp or for the Shop. Various sergeants and the Sergeant Major would check that the rules were carried out. The next night I was sitting in bed reading when the door burst open and The Sergeant Major peered in.

"What are you doing?" he barked.

"Reading a newspaper, Sergeant major," I replied.

"You know it's no lights - don't you?"

"Yes - but I am only using glow-worms."

He peered at me with his shielded torch and played it on the loaded machine gun at my side.

"Glow-worms? Stay there!"

I heard him enter the Battery Office in the house. In a few minutes I heard voices - a woman's voice amongst them. The door opened again.

"Smith - you told the Sergeant Major you had some glow-worms?" It was Oscar - our Major - and his wife. "You claim that you can read a newspaper?"

"Right, Smith - read some local news."

I felt rather foolish as the three of them, in the darkness of the night, watched the little pin-points of light held against the paper. I started reading a report from Chard Cattle market.

"All right Smith - carry on."

"Good night sir - good night madam." I was pleased to ignore the Sergeant Major.

The next day I had an urgent message that I was to move in - with the Bren - to the bedroom with the Office Staff; I even had a spring bed. I had a suspicion that someone must have said that I was going mad and I also had a machine gun.

By the third week in June I had the additional job of acting postman. I had to take all letters, unsealed, to the Officers' Mess for them to censor, then post them later at a local Post Office. Every letter had to have an Officer's signature on the outside - I thereby had an early lesson in forgery but I never discussed military matters in my letters home.

By now, every night, parties of men with pick and shovels would set out by lorry for the coast to dig gun pits. They returned before dawn. I would open the Shop up to sell cigarettes and sweets.

All sorts of rumours abounded and then it was announced that a very senior Officer, probably a General, would visit our position.

I tidied up the shop and wiped over the Bren. I was told to stand at the entrance properly dressed as he passed. He peered at me as he passed and I heard him ask what job I was supposed to do in the Battery.

Within minutes Pullthrough had told me to leave the shop and go to the Stores. There I found that someone had unearthed Reg and the two other H.Q. Specialists and they were trying to sort out all our equipment ready for a move. We were back in business.

As darkness fell that night lorries came up the road and everyone was told to get aboard.

CHAPTER SEVEN

THE FRONTLINE

I was again to discover that one of the most dangerous times for an ordinary soldier was in a Unit movement. At this time the worst traits of the Army would manifest themselves and everyone with any rank would get an almost uncontrollable desire to get the men 'fell in'. Sergeant Majors would wince at the sight of men in an 'untidy heap'. Orders were shouted in the clipped manner of the Parade Ground. So when I had to leave the security of the Battery Shop and the Bren Gun to join a Battery H.Q. lorry that moved out of Aldington to the coast I had a sense of foreboding. It was the last lorry and I did not want to get left behind.

The first streaks of dawn appeared in the eastern sky as I, and my kit, were dumped in a New Romney street. Various sergeants called out groups who quickly straggled off into the darkness. I was alone when I saw that Bombardier Sykes still had the Bren, and I suggested that he recruited me to join two others to get some spades, bags and a pickaxe and walk to the cross-roads. Here we started making a sandbag emplacement under a bush. After a short time he went off to locate the Cookhouse and did not return. The digging was easy and we soon made ourselves a circular hide-out but at about a foot high none of us could remember whether the gun slits should be widest at the inside or outside. After a discussion about old castles and bows and arrows, I volunteered to find some information from a pamphlet we had had back in Devon so I set off to search for Battery Office.

Oscar - our Major - was indeed a man after my own heart. He had abolished all bullshit, all normal parades, and every position had to be hidden. Of course

43

he crept around himself also and often appeared to be in two places at once. He did not tolerate idleness.

So I crept, almost like a badger, quietly and quickly to the central park area and soon, from the shadows, located the Battery Office. But I in my turn was spotted by Oscar himself who sent me scuttling off to a house behind the park - past four 18/25 pounder guns in pits under the sycamore trees. Once there I was ordered to report to Reg, our kindly Specialist sergeant, who reminded me not to do other jobs again - and that included 'running a bloody pub.' Those were strong words from Reg.

The specialists, in the shape of Jim, Harry and myself were soon stripped to the waist, sandbagging the outside of the front bay window. As there had been a very slight drizzle and we were not using clean sand we ourselves quickly became camouflaged. This was to be the Battery Command Post and signallers were bringing in telephone lines from all other positions in New Romney and beyond. Soon a man with a tea bucket arrived and we took a short break inside while Reg told us the glad tidings.

The Battery now had its full complement of three Troops of guns. The four 18/25s in the Park, four 18 pounder Howitzers in houses in the town and four French 75mm Field Guns in a farm two miles back. Every Troop had a Command Post at the guns and an Observation Post. In addition all were to be controlled from our Battery Command Post and from a Battery Observation Post on the sea front at Littlestone. There would be no more matchboxes, no more miniature range - this was the real thing.

Oscar, a small thin man with a piercing eye and red hair, constantly toured the area with a variety of Officers seeing orders were quickly and accurately carried out. As far as we were concerned the Command Post had to be sandbagged outside. The Royal Engineers would call to put timber posts to strengthen the ceiling. There would be a full stand-to for two hours around dusk that night.

Before that every gun would have to be accurately marked on maps. Using the ballistic tables, calculations would have to be made to fire shells 100yds out from the low tide mark after dark. There were special tables for the French guns as they used a different system to ours with quadrants instead of straight degrees. The Command post staff were to sleep in the rooms adjacent to the Post and duty signallers and duty surveyors would be on duty all the time: day and night. Every telephone line would be tested at least once every hour and gunnery calculations would be adjusted every four hours after dark as temperature, pressure and humidity changed. There would be a fully-manned stand-to with Officers one hour either side of dawn and dusk. Men could not walk about exposed to aerial observation in groups larger than pairs. The Cookhouse, just across the Park, would be open all hours of daylight and we could get meals when not actually working at duty station. I got my breakfast at midday - but no one complained.

It was during the early afternoon when the Engineers called to shore up the ceiling that strange events occurred. They soon complained that there was a cellar underneath our floor. Reg called in Lt Pullthrough from the Officers' Mess situated in a big house on the outskirts of the town. They found a locked door and it did not take us long to break it open.

Most of the civilian population, as well as all the Romney Marsh farm livestock, had been evacuated. Before leaving, all the movable furniture and fitting of this house had been moved to the cellar and Pullthrough had soon found a fatigue party of four men to move all this material to the attic.

Pullthrough had found some H.Q. signallers who must have finished their task - or were perhaps inadvertently just taking a short rest at the wrong moment. We four specialists continued to pour over maps and gunnery tables. My special task was to prepare the transparent gun traces used to ensure that all four straddled guns of each Troop ranged on to a single target.

Our work progressed to moans and cursing as various items were banged up the stairs and beyond by our very inexperienced furniture removers. It quickly became apparent that their fatigue was being displaced by an increasing degree of hilarity so that we had later to keep the door shut.

Silence finally took over and we thankfully assumed that Reg could ring up for the Sappers to shore up the floor. Then the door burst open; we all blinked before joining in the laughter. Two of our signallers entered each carrying a crate of bottled Guinness. One was regaled in a long lady's evening dress of dazzling blue with a feathered hat and the other impeccably clad in hunting 'Pink'. They both staggered forward placing their gifts on the end of our tables. They had even brought bottle openers.

Guinness

We four specialists were parched and had long subsisted on Army cocoa. We quickly drank a toast to 'good old 373 Battery' direct from the bottles. Work seemed to get easier, if probably less accurate, after that.

The Sappers, Pullthrough and finally Oscar all joined us in celebration and, as word got out, sundry other personnel found a need to see our maps - and all were permitted without question. By the time the Guinness mine was exhausted the entire Battery was ready to fire. My only fear at the time was that it WOULD fire - just out of sheer joy. Reg was not quite

45

convinced that A Troop's Howitzers would clear the seafront hotels at Littlestone.

The Command post was ready for the full 'stand-to' before dark and I, as duty surveyor that night, had to sit at the table afterwards to convert the 'Meteor Telegrams' and answer any queries coming in. But in quiet moments I could rest or even try to sleep under the table. The signallers took it in turns to man the phones in hourly shifts all night. My friend Bono looked forward to the next day when he predicted that we would all be digging slit trenches at each position - just in case he had a 'special duty'.

The next day we took it in turns with the signallers to dig slit trenches under trees in the back garden. Bono and I managed to locate a few bones in our two man section. The guns were concealed under camouflage nets and a Twin-Lewis Machine Gun graced the churchyard in case an enemy plane became too cheeky. I assumed that someone had got the Bren properly installed by now, even if the slits were the wrong way round.

Popes Hotel

It took us two more days to get the Battery Command Post in full working order. We had also visited all the Troop Posts and the Battery Observation Post in the armoured top lookout of Popes Hotel at Littlestone, from where we could see the distant French coast.

We specialists had not only been trained in the technical Command Post work but also in the work of an Observation Post assistant to the Officer giving the firing orders. We had tables telling how long the shells would take to arrive on target. We also did the work of Officer's assistant at the gun position, checking the targets on a map and seeing that the corrections were given for each gun. The Officer did the shouting but each gun sergeant finally gave the orders to his own gun team.

We all found life very exciting and, just in case we should get bored, Reg worked out a weekly work rota. Each one of us would spend two nights at Popes Hotel, two nights at the Gun Command Post and two nights at the B.C.P. as duty Surveyor. One could be available for sleep.

The glorious summer weather of 1940 would be a good opportunity for swimming in the sea. Reg's solution, after consulting our Officers, was that we four should accurately map every sand dune and beach obstacle along the six mile stretch of coast either side of Littlestone. As Reg pointed out, 'the bloody Hun' would not suspect us of being soldiers if we wore swimming trunks so, with director (small theodolite) and tape measure, we worked in pairs. We had the use of a car to make journeys for meals and visits to the few cafes still open in New Romney. Life again became very pleasant for me and, looking out towards the French coast, I often wondered if the German Army gave such freedom to their technical sergeants to seek the welfare of their men.

By the time this was finished an Order had been given that, in the event of an invasion the Battery would have no retreat but the guns might have to fire in any direction while ammunition lasted. This meant that, apart from firing over open sights, the guns may have to be controlled from any high ground or building back over Romney Marsh.

This meant churches, and I was said to have volunteered to draw panoramic views from the towers of all Romney Marsh churches. Every morning, after 'stand down' I had to collect haversack rations from the Cookhouse and would be dropped off near a church and collected four hours later.,

There were special rules and conditions. I had to have a man with a rifle with me at all times. I never discovered why, as he had no instructions either. Was it, we thought, to see that I did not catch a bus and go home? Was he there to deal with irate Vicars? Or perhaps to see that I did not seduce the Vicarage maidservants? We often wondered - he also had five rounds of ammunition.

The other rule was that we went down to the belfry during air-raid alerts or if we suspected that enemy aircraft could be photographing us.

I had to draw landscapes and mark off every feature likely to be an artillery target and with my prismatic compass mark its exact angle. I was kept very busy. My companion soon became bored with admiring the view and we realised that more than half our time was spent admiring the belfry. As an ex-bellringer his great game was to get all the bells swinging without actually making the slightest tinkle. The ringing of church bells was to be the recognised signal for invasion and I predicted, if he made a mistake, both our deaths by firing squad.

Each day my completed panoramas were used by Reg and the gang who went around the countryside identifying my marked features on the map, and also other features such as cross-roads or buildings in the vicinity.

As soon as this work was finished there came the time for the practice shoot. I happened to have spent the night in the A Troop Command Post so I was ordered to be the Gun Position Officer's assistant.

Our four 4.5 Howitzers were in the front rooms of four houses along the street in New Romney. The front windows and part of the walls to the South had been removed to get the guns in. An exact replica of the front was painted on a replacement boarding with a flap for the muzzle to point out.

The floors had been concreted with a circular rim to take the spades of the guns on recoil. A passage way was build to connect all guns towards the back of the houses and a viewing hole through all the walls so that the Command post could see the guns. We all wore full kit with ear plugs.

After double checking all the figures, angles and dialsight laying of the guns the Officer reported via the signaller "B Troop Ready." The order came down from Oscar from the O.P. at Littlestone for, "A Troop One Round Gunfire. Charge One. Zero 05. 3000y."

In a few seconds the gun sergeants were yelling "Fire!" and an almighty roar was followed by the empty charge cases dropping on the concrete almost like broken cutlery. After a while as the dust cleared we could see from our peephole that each room was a different colour according to distemper used in the decor.

The O.P. was still alive and we waited for the other two troops to fire. Then our turn came again. But this time full charge - all three bags of propellant - to give a flatter curve for the shells.

The 4.5 Howitzer was not anchored to a base platform and so on firing it leapt back against the concrete pad like a steam hammer, shattering the teeth

of the Bombardier gun layer sitting on his little seat.

The Sergeant on No.2 gun was a very resourceful lad who had, I later learnt, come from the garage trade. He had padded this gun spade with a wad of old tyres.

After the most almighty bang and when our brains had settled back in our tin hats we peered through the inspection hole into the brightly coloured mists. Our signaller broke the silence.

"No.2 has gone bloody A.W.O.L., Sir !"

We all peered down the peep hole . It was now clear that the entire gun crew had gone also - as had the wooden front of the room.

"Stop Firing!" shouted our Lieutenant. He had at least followed the rule book.

I now considered it safe to exit into the road. There in the garden across the road was our missing gun with the gun layer still sitting in his little seat. The rest of the crew were frantically trying to manhandle the gun backwards, no doubt to the order 'Without dragropes prepare to retire.' They all had red faces, including their Sergeant. A wonderful shade of vermilion covered them all - and the gun . No 2 Gun had, with the aid of the motor tyres, turned itself into a catapult, but thankfully only after the shell had left for the sea two miles away at Littlestone.

The day shortly arrived when our maps were complete and every possible target had been marked. We all sat for four hours each day just waiting for nothing to happen. Several large boxes of old books had arrived from the WVS and I was picked on by Pullthough to run a lending library for an hour each day.

Reg had, with his usual concern for our welfare, arranged for us to go to the tennis courts on the edge of the town for a couple of hours each afternoon, so that in tin hats, shorts and plimsolls we could at least keep ourselves fit.

After my admonition by the previous Major at Holesworthy I had at first learnt some poetry to avoid frustration from Army stupidity and then decided to become a part-time student. I had now mentioned this to Oscar and with his approval had signed up for a 4 year Agricultural Course with International Correspondence Schools. I thus could sit at my position at Command Post or O.P. and legally study such things as sheep management, soils or muck-spreading. Life had again become very pleasant although we could not get home on leave - and that Reg was working on.

It was in the early afternoon of 10th July while I was walking with Reg to join the other two at the tennis courts when an aeroplane suddenly swooped low over our heads with a roaring engine. I had just noticed the black cross on its side when, out of a clear blue sky, a Spitfire swooped after it. Soon the staccato rattle of machine gun fire ripped at the sky above us - and a small girl screamed further along the Street.

We did not know it at the time but this was to be the very beginning of what was later known as the 'BATTLE OF BRITAIN'. Probably the greatest air show of all time... and we were to have the front seats in the stalls.

CHAPTER EIGHT

Under The Battle Of Britain

We very quickly realised that enemy planes were now using not only cameras but also weapons to try to shoot us. The air-raid sirens would wail out their 'Alerts' all along the coast shortly after dawn and only sounded the 'All-clear' apparently at random during the daylight hours. As this would almost invariably signal the arrival of another plane - either dropping light bombs or spraying bullets - we often wondered if someone was signalling them to come in. There was also the usual rattle of the Battery Lewis Gun and then the arrival of a 'pest-destroying' Spit or Hurricane. The Hurricane was, to our untutored eyes, very similar in shape to the Messerschmidt 109 and we nearly always made our guess from the 'prone' position - just in case we were wrong.

It now appeared that Hitler had temporarily given up the idea of a quick invasion in favour of an air battle. This did greatly upset our recreation periods as the battles usually took place after our dinner. Not only did our tennis suffer as we had to spend some time during a game lying, semi-naked, except for tin hat, shorts and plimsolls, either side of the net - but we often forgot the score and had to start again. Furthermore, if bombs were fairly near and we were not actually at our post we

Fifteen - Love?

had to lie in the garden slit trenches - by order of Oscar. It appeared that our Officers did not know about tennis.

I had been forbidden to use white paper to continue my farming course while lying in the trenches, as an Officer said I would reveal our presence to the enemy. I solved this by doing my work on Army khaki shit-house paper. This in turn started the rumour that the specialists took fright easily. To be seen carrying toilet paper around under fire was not, I gathered, in the 'best traditions of the Service'.

At night, in the little armour-plated lookout tower at the top of Popes Hotel at Littlestone we could watch the flashing of the big German guns at Cap Griz Nez shooting across the Channel. The Royal Engineer surveyors in the room below would take angles and fix the position so that our Wellington Bombers would rumble over and drop bombs that would even shake our windows on this side. I enjoyed the O.P. work and in the darkness a captain or even Oscar himself would often join the line signaller and myself to chat about civilian life. The battery wireless signaller was on a roof several hundred yards away so that he could see us being blown up in the first few minutes of an invasion and so get another O.P. to take over.

The bar at the hotel was open in the evening and we would have a drink before climbing the 120 steps into the roof. The Officer would have a proper hotel bedroom to sleep over night and I was allowed to get some sleep - fully clothed - on a settee by the door. The signaller could get some sleep with his headphones on - only to be woken up every hour by Battery H.Q.

The hotel bar was often occupied by the colourful members of a Commando Unit - each wearing his old Unit's uniform - who claimed to go over in the night and slit German throats. They called us 'armchair soldiers' although I did explain to one proud Scot that I was not really a soldier at all but just wore the uniform. I recall that he was sharpening his knife at the time. I had by now devised a way of doing my farming studies on duty and carried my pamphlets and a supply of toilet paper inside my battle dress.

Most of us got quite used to the 'ping' of spent bullets off the roads or against the trees or buildings. We managed to actually lie flat before the odd bombs, whistling down, had exploded; we believed the old artillery adage that 'you don't hear the shell that kills you', although plainly no one had been able to confirm this accurately. But when the last of a stick of six bombs brought a whole plate-glass shop window outwards onto the pavement beside me as I lay in the gutter, a colleague a few yards away shouted to me not to look upwards as the plane would have been sure to spot my ashen-white face. That was good thinking. I was waiting for the seventh bomb - which did not arrive.

On the afternoon of the 13th August the four of us were playing tennis under clear blue skies and a warm sun. The air-raid sirens had again sounded all along the coast for, we suspected, an enemy plane looking for shipping in the Channel. After a time we could hear the pulsating drone of many engines gradually coming nearer. We could make out a faint grey patch of smoke far to the south.

Soon we could make out a mass formation of bombers - flying straight and slowly directly inland. We reckoned about sixty and the tiny glinting sparks that appeared around them were the fighters. High above - each one at the end of a white silken vapour trail - were other formations of fighters showing as tiny dots.

As they came over the coast-line the shrill whistle of a bomb sent us all diving for the net. We waited until the 'WOOOMPH' shook the air and the few seconds that would be required for the iridescent fragments of black metal to spray the surrounding area. We quickly gazed out over the wheat field adjoining at the puff of smoke rising into the almost still air.

"Must be No. 1 bomber ranging," was Reg's verdict. Like artillery setting their ranges the bombers must be setting their bombsights - for almost without exception every formation of enemy bombers let a random bomb go just a few miles inland.

When the formation was just overhead we could now see other silken trails coming to meet them from inland. Anti-Aircraft guns either side of the marsh around Hythe and Rye had opened up and black puffs of smoke lingered in the distance.

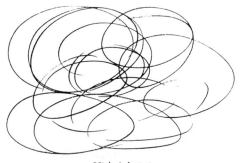
Hitler's knitting

It wasn't long before the rattle of machine guns shattered the sunlit sky and the silken threads began to knit themselves in circular patterns; like a passing thunderstorm and an angry swarm of bees the seething mass moved northwards. Then some planes broke out of the bottom of the mass, smoke poured out, tracking them downwards. A couple of planes continued down with screaming engines to strike the ground like a shell. White parachutes lingered in the sky, very slowly drifting in the gentle breeze.

We watched, spellbound as the whole airshow moved away in the distance. We had just decided to resume our tennis when the first returning enemy plane screamed down over us and out to sea at low level. First the fighters - low on fuel and ammunition we suspected - some still being chased by our planes. Then the bombers - every plane for itself - just releasing any surplus bombs before they reached the coast. Our fighters were using their ammunition to good effect: we could actually see gashes in the enemy's wings and tails - when we felt it safe to gaze skywards.

In the scramble back home to France the enemy planes obviously did not see anything worth aiming at in New Romney or Littlestone. We assumed that they must have thought that a few 'holiday makers' on a tennis court were no military threat. Reg was of the opinion that, if he asked if we could dig slit trenches by the courts, our Officers would have ordered us to put on proper uniform and use the official trenches in the town.

So for a few days more I was able to watch the air battles and we considered it just as safe as in the town. The largest formation consisted of over three hundred enemy bombers. The ranging bombs had killed some civilians and one had fallen between us and the Officers' Mess - in fact we at first thought that it had scored a direct hit.

As the air battles increased in size and fury more debris was raining down. Bits of fuselage swished down like waste paper. Planes did most strange aerobatics with smoke pouring from them before diving into the Marsh. Some planes would circle around visibly without a pilot gradually getting lower. Parachutes seemed to linger for ages before drifting to earth. Some bombs exploded in the bombers. There were human bodies tumbling down to break up like china ornaments or splash into soggy ground. Out across the Marsh we could see damaged planes with flames and smoke pouring out of them.

The whole sky seemed to be filled with vapour trails ("Hitler's knitting") for hours after the last plane had been grounded or escaped. The air-raid sirens would then sound the 'all-clear' just in time for a few single low level enemy planes to do a reconnaissance.

After the air battles the RAF would send lorries out across the Marsh. They would collect our own pilots who might have parachuted down or survived a crash amongst the anti-landing poles placed across any potential safe landing strip. Bodies had to be collected as well as bits or even whole damaged planes. It soon became apparent that the spoil of battle could be collected and any member of the Battery who could get hold of a vehicle could join in the fun.

Many drivers soon sported enemy binoculars, watches and bits of uniform. This accounted for a Command Post signaller turning up after midnight, when I was duty surveyor, dressed as Hitler and giving the enemy salute. Our ration lorry driver developed a macabre sense of humour and had been known to take bits of badly roasted enemy pilots via the Cookhouse to the New Romney Mortuary. While the air battles were still on the Battery must have felt confident that a land attack had been abandoned. Limited home leave was started and, in the first list, I was able to travel west to Somerset and see the huge number of wrecked planes littering the south eastern fields beside the railway lines south of London.

I had a week to get back to farming. I now shot rabbits driven out by Pogey, my pet ferret, with whom I felt an ever-growing affinity. A small field of oats was ready for harvest. I worked hard and with relish - I was really happy as a manual worker again. I think my mother had feared that I would not return. There were evacuees lodging at the farm and also a schoolgirl called Monica, with a great love of cows, would spend part of her school holidays at the farm since her parents were stranded in Egypt.

Back in New Romney we were on duty every night for the 'stand to' period either side of darkness. I was also encouraged to take a signals course and to learn to drive lorries and Quad gun tractors. I had to conceal that I already had a civilian driving licence and had to avoid the Army testing exam as I would have been found out - the Army issued red Civilian Licences. This course, which I did three times, enabled me to get a lift along the coast road towards Dover and the 'TOWN IS NOW BEING SHELLED' signs. The sergeant in charge would not let me drive on the last course and I dropped off at Dymchurch to play on the dodgems. I would catch a bus back. On one occasion I had just left and was only a hundred yards away when a bomb wrecked the whole centre of Dymchurch.

Although the main bombing was at night in London, single planes almost constantly searched the coastal areas for targets. There was one scare of invasion when a yellow haze was seen in the Channel and we stayed at the ready at outposts for a whole week.

Then the Infantry started mining the beach, the gardens and the roadsides, and much of the fun went out of our stay. A Bofors anti-aircraft gun was brought in to defend the town but it was bombed after two days. Oscar must have realised that many of us were weary and a little disheartened. Even our machine gunner reckoned that time was going too slowly and had, so he claimed, shot the hands off the church clock.

Oscar's answer was dramatic. Every man was given a rifle and ammunition and was allowed to shoot at any enemy plane if they wished. Although the standard Lee-Enfield rifle was heavy to fire upwards, the resulting 'pheasant shoot' meant that, at last, enemy planes were welcomed. I reckoned that even the solitary seagull was not absolutely safe.

Then something happened in early November that seemed to shake us to our roots. It was announced that we were leaving. We were given three days to check all positions, clean everything up and pack our personal kit. An escape hole had been opened, and although I was given a hint by one of the Officers that we were going for a 'rest', even the most placid of us seemed a little frightened.

It was at stand-to on Guy Fawkes' night 1940 that every man was in his battle position in full battle order with his kit nearby. It was most eerie. We were told exactly what to do. I was at the survey table in the Battery Command Post as No. 4 surveyor with all my traces and maps in front of me. I wore the Drakes Drum shoulder flash of the 45th Infantry Division.

Quite silently my replacement - wearing the Black Cat shoulder flash - appeared in the doorway. I stood up and couldn't resist just shaking his hand and wishing him well as he settled in my seat. I quickly gathered my kit and there, in the darkness, was the waiting lorry. When it was full we made our way to Ashford where in a station hall we were given a bag of food, filled our water bottles and within the half hour the entire Battery was there, some 250 men. The train was waiting.

A short delay while bombs dropped locally had shaken the windows and the A.A. Fire outside the town had ceased and, docile, we climbed aboard. There was no excitement and no one had much to say. Soon the train pulled out of the station going north and I quickly nodded off to sleep like all the others around me.

CHAPTER NINE

YORKSHIRE, TIME TO REST

Military trains are like stopping trains without stations, for our slow, punctuated journey went on most of the night. By dawn we were finally disembarked and lorried to a number of Chapel Halls in the joint mining villages of Mapplewell and Staincross, villages as large as their names and gathered around the shaft of Barnsley Main Colliery. The buildings were blackened like a miner's face, in sharp contrast to the warmth of our welcome.

After settling into my allotted space, with three blankets on a bare floor, I set out with Jim, my specialist colleague, to the fish and chip shop. We finished up eating it with knife and fork in front of a blazing coal fire. We were already adopted 'sons' with an open invitation to look in any evening.

After my first full night's sleep for many months I obeyed the Battery notice pinned to the door and joined the parade of Battery H.Q. personnel at 09.00 the next morning. We were instructed to wear overalls, which gave us a sort of anonymity. Probably because, I innocently thought, one of our Officers had already noticed that large hovering pieces of soot slowly descended from the atmospheric gloom as we walked along the pavements.

The Battery Sergeant Major, who had been deprived of his full glory in Kent, was now able to 'do his stuff'. Lt Pullthrough had attended this parade, apparently just to issue the magic words 'Carry on, Sergeant Major', before disappearing to join the other Officers. The parade was not well attended and our S.M. divided the rabbits equally amongst the five Sergeants attending, each group being marched away into the fog in different directions.

Six of us were marched in straggling order to a small hut, overshadowed by the mountainous colliery main waste tip. A miner produced a sledge hammer for each of us, and we - rather like the proverbial prisoners of Dartmoor - were instructed to break up the great limestone blocks around us into some sort of road stone. Having been chained to a desk by the Army for many months I rather enjoyed this fresh activity; although, from my farm experience, group stone-cracking like this could be the most dangerous thing I had yet done in the Army, for we wore neither tin hats nor goggles. For the first time I was rather enjoying the freedom of being an Army rabbit. Stone-cracking certainly released my pent-up feelings - I believed I was rather good at stone cracking.

By now my dislike of being a proper soldier had, I knew, become widely known to a number of the Officers. I suspected that to avoid conflict with the Sergeant Major they put me deliberately on solitary jobs. So I was not surprised that after a very few minutes a clerk, carrying a bit of paper, was telling our Sergeant that I was wanted immediately in the Battery Office.

I arrived, suitably grimed, to find Lt. Pullthrough and the Sergeant Major inspecting a large flat piece of white cardboard. I think the S.M. winced a little as I had tied a piece of string below each knee - in the manner that old farm workers did to prevent rats causing trouble during threshing. But in my case it was to prevent my oversize overalls dragging on the ground.

"Ah Smith!" said Pullthrough as I attempted some sort of a salute. "We want you to ink in a list down one side here of every job in the Battery. So that every man can have his name pencilled in. It's got to be done neatly," he added, "it'll hang outside the Battery Commander's door." The S.M. eyed me very suspiciously. He handed me the Battery Complement list that we had always kept in the Kent Command Post.

I never felt at ease in the presence of Sergeant Majors but I thought it a good idea to try my old Devon gambit. I deliberately spoke to Pullthrough.

"Can I find somewhere to do this job? It'll take a bit of space. Sir."

"What had you in mind?" said Pullthrough.

"I could work in the canteen that some of the ladies have for us up the road, sir?" I suggested.

"Right! Go ahead then. You must be ready with the names tomorrow afternoon."

I left the Office carrying the biggest bit of 'paper' in the Battery. Depositing my overalls at my bed space and collecting my pens and Indian ink I soon negotiated with the ladies to use a table in their canteen: and my 'masterpiece' was completed on time. The Battery Clerk had given me a list of personnel for me to pencil in. I did the whole lettering in an oriental type of freehand script which was, I judged, very civilian.

I noticed that there was a place for 'The Battery Surveyor'. So I put myself in this space as this was a 'trade' job - and all tradesmen and permanent staff were normally exempt from parades in the Artillery.

When I presented the completed board at the office I was given a list of those on leave, away on courses or posted away. So I immediately had to set about deleting names or reinserting them elsewhere. It seemed that about a third of the Battery were away. I was the only specialist left at times, and as the regular office staff refused to do my sort of lettering I was ordered by the S.M. to report each morning after Parade, armed with a rubber and pencil to bring the list up to date before the Major arrived.

It was then that I realised that I had made a mistake and myself very conspicuous.

While I was in Kent I had the job of marking the individual gun positions in a small book of tracing paper. As I sat in the Command Post doing this I had used my spare time to do caricatures of Battery members, from the Colonel downwards, on the tracing paper of a spare book. I had marked my fake book of gun traces with the usual official notice 'That the contents must not be communicated to unauthorised persons'. In the move this book had gone 'absent without leave' and it was not with the few Command Post documents in the Battery Office. I was worried - very worried.

A few days later when I was creeping into the Battery Office to do the day's 'casualty' list the S.M. was waiting for me.

"Get your hat on straight!" he almost shouted at me; "You're wanted in the Battery Commander's Office at once - follow me."

When we arrived there he knocked on the door and I followed him in.

"Gunner Smith - Sir!" he snapped, as his heels clicked together.

To my horror it was not Oscar I faced but the Regimental Adjutant. A regular Major: a large red faced man with a slight stutter and famed for his vile temper.

I stood in front of his desk and saluted. In front of him on the desk was my book of caricatures. He looked at the S.M., looked at me, picked up the book, slowly opened it to the drawing of the Colonel and laid it down open on his desk in front of him.

"Are these your d-drawings, Smith?" he said.

The next half minute went very slowly as my voice seemed to have disappeared into my boots and the thoughts of field punishments flashed before my mind. I was gradually getting smaller and I could sense the Sergeant Major's eyes drilling into me. He was also in the book - complete with horns and a tail. I wondered if my pals would be on the firing squad ...

The Adjutant broke the silence. His voice was strangely not stern. He turned over another page as he spoke.

"We've d-decided," he hesitated. "that these are very good -Smith. We shall have to appoint you B-Battery Artist. Sergeant Major, we have a job for him - the kit layouts."

The Adjutant handed me my book back and I did one of my very bad salutes as I escaped out of the door followed by the S.M.

"What you have got to do," he explained, "is to do thirty copies of a new kit layout to be pinned up in every billet in the Regiment. Right - go back to your own kit and lay it out properly. I will come up and inspect it in half an hour with the Orderly Sergeant."

I wasn't out of the wood yet for I always

"Are these your drawings?"

contrived to be on some form of night duty so my kit was only laid out for sleeping - and my blankets never seemed to be square for a start.

So for the next half hour by a frantic process of minor substitution from neighbouring kits I managed to present a perfectly laid out kit with even my own name on the kitbag. After minor adjustments I was left to do a drawing from which to prepare the copies.

It was at this stage that a group of my H.Q. colleagues arrived back and I had a lot of explaining to do; that I, the most unsoldierlike member of the Battery, was to do the new kit layout and had got the S.M. to approve. When I arrived back at the hall well after 'lights out' that night I found that my entire bed, complete with kitbag between the blankets, had been dragged to the middle of the floor and labelled 'The Queen of Sheba'. I never quite discovered why ...

I used the hostility towards my part in this piece of Regimental bullshit to arrange for me to work in the house of my 'adopted' parents for the next three weeks. Both were school teachers and he was, I later discovered, the Captain of the local Home Guard. His younger sister, Margaret, kept house for them and kept me supplied with refreshments as I drew up the kit layout - drawn on an imaginary magic carpet. I even had my civilian clothes sent up. This was my idea of soldiering.

I was sent on a week's leave when the job was completed and on my return I found that our specialist sergeant Reg and three others had left to form a Survey Team at Regimental Headquarters. Several Officers had also left.

There was the usual crisis to get volunteers to become specialists. As a group

Adjutant

we were despised as racketeers and skivers - which was, of course, not without justification, and I was thought to have brought this to a fine art. There was a considerable stigma to be fighting a War with a slide rule, a set of logarithm tables, a tape measure and a sharp pencil and masses of maps.

There was a rule in the Wartime Army that anyone being absent from his Unit for more than three weeks - either through illness (which included VD infection) or even in military prison - forfeited the right to return to his old unit, and they supplied a reservoir to replace battle casualties. As I filled in the jobs chart each morning I soon realised that we were getting short staffed. Being a combat unit we all had to be medical grade A1 and several men and Officers had, I knew, failed to pass. Others seemed to have just been posted away - often at an hour's notice. I felt insecure.

We specialists had lost our sergeant and three men to the new Regimental H.Q. Survey Party. There were only two of us left who had been in Kent. So when I had to mark Sid up as a two-stripe Bombardier and two new men had been persuaded to volunteer for training I suspected my 'civilian' holiday was near an end.

As soon as I presented my completed 30 copies of kit layout at the Battery Office I went home for a week's leave. On my return all Specialists and a few reluctant volunteers were lorried each day to a school in Barnsley for a two-week course. We sat at desks and took notes of 'procedures' for all activities from recording targets and shell fire at an Observation Post to recording and checking that the four guns of each troop kept on line to the working out of creeping barrages and night firing calculations. We were always armed with a 'bit of paper'. I felt I was at last being properly trained for the job. We were in future to do a lot less pure survey and to concern ourselves with being assistants to all the Officers, which meant that we would not be available for fatigues or the attentions of the Sergeant Major.

B.S.M.

By now the Battery seemed to have reclaimed its guns. Four 18 pounders, four old Howitzers and the four antique French 75 mm. This meant using three different sets of calculations. We also now had a set of vehicles so I was not surprised when we were told to prepare for a journey in convoy to the firing ranges on

North Yorkshire Blubberhouse Moor. They had found a new job for the four of us. With one of the new Officers we were to go ahead to Grassington village and arrange for all the Battery to sleep in sheds, huts or anywhere we could find. The Officers would find a hotel.

Our Officer was a 'sixth former' type, very young and newly commissioned, who was obviously not quite aware of the devious nature of the troops. It was just before dark when the list I had given them was completed and all the men had been found somewhere to sleep - except the four of us. I had given them the fatigue list from which we were deleted. Our Officer went with us to the cinema to arrange for us to sleep behind the screen on stage.

During the day we would go in convoy to the Moor. But the drizzle and fog never lifted, so we just sat around in our lorries until dark when we would return to Grassington bedraggled and wet - we had a mobile cookhouse on the Moor. To add to our discomfort we had to be blasted by the last house of the cinema... shivering with our blankets behind the screen.

This was our last effort for on our return several men got pneumonia and there were the usual parades and sundry drill sessions. Sid was now a sergeant and with some brilliance he arranged for us to meet each day at the Miner's Institute - the 'Stute' - for snooker and dominoes. He even arranged for the four of us to go to a private house for cheesecake and tea at regular break periods, and I was even relieved of my daily visit to the Battery Office.

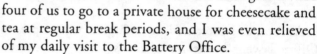

We never knew what prompted the Army to try to tighten up general discipline but, as the snows of winter melted and we were considered to have been sufficiently rested we were told to gather up all the kit and make for Colchester. We were to go into Barracks.

New skills

CHAPTER TEN
CONFINED TO BARRACKS

Probably to atone for the often undisciplined pleasures of our Yorkshire rest-period the Battery was sentenced to a spell in Regular Army Barracks. Officially we were to re-equip at Le Cateau Barracks in Colchester.

Barracks are the den of the Army beast. For it is here that it confines the young human male and, trying to captivate his mind and body, mould him into a 'soldier': obedient to the command, unthinking in action and whose reflexes are conditioned by known stimuli. The atmosphere of this Barracks was distinctly early Victorian; everything in dead straight lines, the high surrounding walls echoing the shouted commands and the crash of many boots on acres of tarmac. The subdued ornateness of the roofs concealed the unrelieved monotony of the interiors. It was stark, severe and unyielding.

Guards on the main gate were erect and impassive; their only possible function was to salute officers, for they were only armed with pickaxe handles.

The Battery was not operational. Our guns and vehicles were lined up in rows so that they could be polished, inspected, re-polished and re-inspected.

There was a strict segregation of Officers, sergeants and men which mitigated against our being a fighting unit. There was, as a colleague observed: "Bugger all to do except bullshit!"

We slept in large rooms with three blankets on a small palliasse we stuffed with straw. There were no chairs or tables and the lighting was so poor that reading was difficult. A canteen was open for limited hours and sold little but 'gaspers, wads and char'. The tables were all used for housy-housy in the evenings. I found life restricted and desperate.

The days were, we gathered, to be devoted to inspections and marching and rifle drill with a period of physical training. All this on the now sacred Barrack Square. In the evenings those on punishments - known as 'confined to Barracks' - would be given an hour's spell of marching drill in full kit, so that all could see.

The town was patrolled by Military Police to enforce 'lights out' and see all were correctly saluting and properly dressed. As Army legend relates, they were 'seeking those whom they could devour and whose red headgear resembled the flowing of the blood of the innocents.'

Jim - our specialist sergeant - seeing our plight, had a word to one of our Officers and put his 'plan A' into operation. As our skills were not required he found the four of us a 'technical' job in the vast Barrack cookhouse.

While the rest of our colleagues prepared for their ration of Bullshit the next morning we reported to a sergeant in the vast dining room. Adjoining it was a room with a machine that somewhat resembled a farm threshing machine. There were drive belts and handles - moving platforms - and electric motors. It was a special military plate washer.

We had its working explained to us - quite a simple beast to operate.

We stacked it up with piles of plates from the shelves and turned on

The Plate Cracker

the spray jets and motors. As the room filled with steam we had to observe it from the doorway. The plates did not need drying for they were too hot to handle. This was rather fun - somewhat like driving an early tank.

By the second day we were developing our skills and calculated that if we doubled up the load, increased the water flow and manually assisted the grinding electric motors we could complete our morning's work in little more than an hour. Likewise we could clear the plates in half that time after tea. We reckoned that our method gave only about 2% breakages but this could be concealed. Strangely the regular staff at the cookhouse did the midday dinner washing-up.

The problem of filling in our spare time then became our chief concern. I had taken some books along to the canteen out of hours and ended up with an

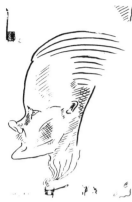

hour's road-sweeping. We could get tea from the cookhouse and we did not relish sitting around there all day - it seemed insuperable.

The solution was found by running along to the Town Swimming Baths. Here was a haven free from the Military Police and in just bathing trunks we could laze around admiring the scenery and the few females who tested the waters. We became very sun-tanned. Luckily the weather was kind.

My sojourn in the cookhouse confirmed the theory that, for every one soldier that actually fights, there are nineteen soldiers who see he stays there. The permanent staff, at all levels, are totally exempt from all parades, drill and weapon training. They are a sort of sub-culture into which our own permanent staff -including Sid, our storeman, and the clerks, cookhouse staff, including General, and the Shit House Wallah - were absorbed. There were also the repair staff, including our Staff-Sergeant mechanic. In addition there were the batmen, or Officer's servants who rarely left the Officer's quarters. There were also a number of drivers. There were I gathered Officers in charge and also a range of permanent N.C.O.s.

Lurking around the Barracks were presumably General's 'hewers'. They came with the dusk and offered their dubious knee-trembling services for two shillings. It must have been presumed that many carried the 'pox' for a list of men losing all their efficiency pay would appear on the notice board. There was also an 'E.T.' hut where men wishing to consort with these ladies could obtain free 'french letters' and an anti-bacterial powder only after signing their names in the book provided. They would afterwards be exempt from suffering pay deductions if they caught the pox. The ladies could be visually graded into those seeking Officers, sergeants and the men. 'Hewers' apparently operated their own class system.

As usual after a spell of 'unemployment' there would be a scramble to get our survey kit sorted and to find enough specialists to go round. There should have been two at each troop - the command post and the O.P. - and four at Battery H.Q. command post and one for the Battery Major's O.P., making eleven in all. Since the very beginning we had lost over twenty specialists to greater things. Most of these had left for Officer training and others to form the Regimental Survey Party; others left because they were needed back in civilian life or because they had special skills for technical Units - the Ordnance Corps, Service Corps or Royal Engineers. Three early specialists had joined gun crews and two were now sergeants, while a third was a very popular Troop Sergeant Major.

Even the Army could not make a man do sums or take notes at a lecture - so they tried bribery, on which I thrived. There were periods when I was not needed - and I always feared that one day I would have to start to be a traditional soldier. The notice boards had been full of requests for special skills.

Gun Sergeant

The call came after three weeks at Colchester and we moved out in convoy at dawn to have another strange experience - we were to be stationed in a disused furniture factory in High Wickham. There was no parade ground and we had to be ready to move at a moment's notice.

We had gone 'Mobile'.

CHAPTER ELEVEN
GETTING MOBILE

In my early days General had explained to us how, in War, a unit would suffer continual casualties. I had wrongly assumed that these would be battle losses but we in the West Somerset Yeomanry had not suffered from any enemy action, yet men - of all ranks - just seemed to disappear. They just appeared on the Battery Orders as 'Posted'. I always had the fear that I would suddenly, at even a few minutes' notice, find myself in another strange unit.

After two years I really thought I had this Unit taped.

In 1941 we found ourselves living in Large's vacant furniture factory in High Wickham. We used a small office on the second floor as the 'Command Post'. Jim, our sergeant, was very quiet and calculating and, like Reg before him, could usually get his way with the H.Q. Officers. We were the only original H.Q. specialists remaining. Art, a lithe little fellow, had now been persuaded to join us from the signallers. Then a new man had arrived from some other Battery. He was rather loud in his manner - and I had the first impression that he had fallen foul of his first Sergeant Major and perhaps even ended up in the 'glasshouse'. He seemed to lack the craftiness of the ferret, but I was soon to learn he had some very interesting ideas.

We had our first breakfast, cooked on mobile stoves in the factory yard, and had been told by Jim to be in the C.P. at 09.00hrs. We checked in the equipment - large rangefinder, director, marker stakes, tapes, writing

equipment and slide rules, a mountain of maps, pamphlets and gunnery forms. Also a couple of plain survey tables and white sheets of paper.

Jim had great news for us. Both of the Command Post Officers had left, which normally didn't matter a lot as we rarely saw them. Two new officers had arrived. The Command Post had always been a sort of bolthole where we could escape. We were now in for a shock.

We four sat around the table. Jim was just explaining that we had no orders for that day so we would sort the equipment and do a little cleaning of lenses. I had a book on pig-keeping in front of me and was getting another gun trace book ready for doing some new caricatures. The door suddenly burst open - we started to struggle to our feet as we realised it was a strange Officer.

"Carry on" he exclaimed as he threw his officer's hat on the table and pulled up a chair. "I'm your new Command Post Officer - Mr Taylor."

He was a tall powerfully built man with the shadow of a sergeant's stripes still on his battle dress. He gave us each a kindly and knowing smile as Jim introduced each of us. He was the first Officer I had ever seen who appeared to be enjoying himself. He reminded me of a jolly cowboy.

His assistant would be over from the Mess shortly he explained and in a few minutes we were joined by what was to be the straight man of a comedy team. We christened them Blanco Bill and Mr Rumble - it suited them.

Mr Rumble also bore the sergeant's stripe marks on his battle-dress and we learnt was also an ex-specialist. Both had escaped from Dunkirk.

'Rumble'

During the rest of that day we were treated to tales of the Blitzkrieg and how efficient we would have to be to beat the Hun. Blanco assured us that if we lost this War all young men would be castrated and used as slave labourers. Rumble was obviously a much milder man who must have been quite like our Sergeant Jim before he did his three months' officer training course. He told us his documents had been mislaid and he had been discovered at his home on 'accidental' leave for six weeks before being posted.

During the course of the day I had returned my pig book to inside my battle dress blouse and had managed to get a good smiling likeness of Blanco on a gun trace sheet. But our new Officer had obviously been forearmed about his new team and demanded to see what I had been scribbling - no action was to be taken if I did a copy for his girlfriend.

So for the next week we assembled in the Command Post where he would check that we knew all the latest gunnery procedures, both at the Command Posts and at the observation posts. Blanco had also shaken up the signallers, the drivers and even had a word with the gun crews. He was devastatingly efficient and polite. Winning the War was going to be great fun.

Our spies said he was not popular in the Officers' Mess for we were an old Yeomanry Regiment of more rigid class distinctions. To sit down in the Command Post and chat to the 'men' was not done. We wondered how he would take to having a properly laid out Mess table with a white table cloth while on manoeuvres. Did he realise that Officer promotion in our Unit was on seniority? How would he take to Major Oscar having his wife and private car joining in the Battery Convoy? How would he deal with the new regular Battery Sergeant Major - who was glimpsed, with gleaming boots and a bull neck, on parade for the first time that morning?

We were to have the new 25-pounder guns and a full set of vehicles. We were to be prepared to move in convoy to anywhere in Britain at a few hours' notice. 'Mobile' meant what it said.

High Wickham had been the centre of the furniture-making industry but had been transferred to 'secret' work for the War. Being fairly near London we were not welcomed by the 'natives' as had been our experience in rural Devon and Yorkshire.

But we were certainly welcomed into the night by a bevy of women in scant clothing, short skirts, mostly dyed-golden curls and covered in scent. They demanded a two-shilling service fee from ordinary soldiers. These were indeed the 'hewers' about which we had been alerted by General. We even had a short lecture by the M.O. on the dangers of picking up V.D., for these were the professional prostitutes moving out from the London Blitz. The evenings were often a great problem as the last meal was about 18.00 hrs; we could then just laze about on our beds, go to a pub and make a pint last all evening or run the gauntlet of the streets. We only received about four shillings a week pay and a pint would cost nearly sixpence.

Our first problem was with the new Battery Sergeant Major. He insisted on his moment of morning glory when we would all parade for the respective sergeants - signallers, drivers, gun teams - to march us all away after the magical command from a junior Officer, 'Carry on, Sergeant Major'. I got

69

screamed at by that person for not doubling out of the ranks and I was given an instruction that the Crown of the Sergeant Major's Sleeve was put there by the King. I was the only specialist on parade that day so I just shouted "All present!" when the specialists were called and just walked away. I should have apparently doubled and then shouted the order to dismiss myself. The Army I hated was still alive and lurking.

The next day Blanco Bill dashed into the Command Post to announce, with his usual great delight, that a Big Battle was planned. The whole 55th Wessex Division of some fifteen thousand men was to meet the 'enemy' coming down from the North of England. We would have to stow all our equipment in the 15cwt 'Y' Truck and he with four of us and the driver would be the Battery advance party. He would be given the 'secret' map reference early next day. We would then drive to somewhere in the Midlands and arrange for the guns, vehicles and the personnel to arrive after dark and put up for the night for the battle to commence at dawn.

Blanco was in his element and imbued us with his infectious humour. The map reference was somewhere 200 miles to the north east. There were no signposts so Blanco map read the whole way. We only stopped for 'piss stops' of a few minutes about every hour with the driver exercising his 'Yeomanry' prerogative of watering the front wheel. We ate our rations as we went along and I drove part of the way, going as fast as the old Bedford Truck would go - fifty mph on the level.

The map reference would be at a road junction and here we erected the Battery code sign - a red and blue painted old fuel can with the code 42 cut out to be illuminated by an internal hurricane lantern after dark. We would go down the side road and our first job, according to Blanco, was to find a large farm house, for our Officers to rest and sleep that night.

Ideally the cows or cattle would then be turned out of a large shed for the men to sleep on straw. The garage would be the command post with a Tilley light on all night. The guns would be parked under trees or camouflaged around the farm as would the gun tractors and vehicles. Drivers would sleep in or under their vehicles. Every position had to be selected and marked in daylight and we had to take people around after dark. The final job was to mark the Battery men's 'latrine' with a large white peg. The gun crews would then later dig a long trench and place a long pole along the middle. The specialist who had given Blanco the most trouble during the day would be pointedly given the white peg in a little ceremony - more to amuse than punish. I would frequently get this job due to my interest in using the Battery Range finder for bird watching in the woods or straying to examine badger

BATTERY COMMAND POST

holes. One night I had found a live hedgehog and was using it as a paper weight on the C.P. desk just when Blanco ushered the Brigadier around. They were not amused .... another white peg!

After fixing and marking all the positions we would rest a little and after dark we would all pile in 'Y' truck and go back to the junction and with our now lighted sign await the convoy. Blanco would see that our truck was camouflaged under a net and then take it upon himself to entertain us with tales of his life in the Regular Army. A sort of sanitised version of the traditional class distinction, stupidity and near brutality, according to General, who was now a bombardier in charge of the cookhouse area.

The 45th Infantry Division on the move meant some fifteen thousand men in vehicles and, in the stillness of the night, they could be heard some ten miles away, rather like the buzzing of the big formations of German bombers assembling over the French Channel coast. Finally the dipped lights of the leading vehicle would arrive. Oscar and the HQ vehicles, with the BSM on his motorbike, would follow Blanco Bill, in 'Y' Truck, away down the lanes. Our sergeant would jump on the running board of a leading vehicle as Blanco's first job was to see the Officers' Mess was fixed and there was the Command Post to set up with Mr Rumble.

We four specialists took a Troop, of four guns and vehicles each, with the odd specialist ensuring that the cooks got to their allocated spot. I always had the fear that I would miss a turning and get lost, for without signposts and with only the shielded headlights of the leading vehicles for illumination landmarks were difficult to see.

We would only get a few hours' rest. I would often sleep by myself on hay or straw under the roof of a

The White Peg

Dutch barn. We would move out in battle formation to get the guns fixed and ready for 'firing' at dawn. Blanco and Rumble were deadly efficient and we soon learnt to move at the double. I usually prepared the gun traces for the twelve guns and would then have to accompany Oscar to the forward Observation Post to do the panorama and plot the troop positions on his maps ready to do 'battle'.

The idea was to leapfrog each troop forward separately with the OPs and command posts moving and working at the same time. Although we used to

71

get very tired, and also hungry, it was great fun. Oscar often used to share his well-prepared sandwiches and coffee with me as I could not be spared to leave the O.P. although the Officers would change.

I often stayed at an OP all day, without a break, with several different more senior Officers. Perhaps the next day I would manage to stay at the Battery Command Post or even be lent to one of the Troops. I was used to replace specialist 'casualties'.

To add to the Battery problems the Army, realising that men worked better in a job they liked, regularly advertised for skilled men to apply for trade jobs - if they had not reached to rank of full sergeant. But so far no one had use for a farm worker or rabbit catcher.

I was by now well known for the tricks I would constantly play on the Army. I always carried a spare unmarked uniform and had been known to go out to a pub at the lull in a 'battle'. Two of us even had a bath, a hotel dinner, and we finished the evening with a pint after going to a film. One evening on manoeuvres we found ourselves sitting behind Blanco himself who even had a girl with him. At the pay parade on our return to base he had publicly asked me in front of all the Battery how I had the cheek to draw pay as well. I had replied that after all he got paid himself, did he not? The S.M. began to explode.

During the next few months we went all over the southern counties. Essex, Suffolk, Norfolk, Cambridgeshire, Wiltshire. We furnished Y1 Truck with its own camp beds and cooking utensils and we often cooked meals as we went along, usually beans or cheese on toast. On one occasion Y Truck stopped suddenly in Bulford and our stove flared up to catch fire to the camouflage netting stored around us in the back. We were regularly passing Military Police as we beat out the flames without daring to stop. We still had beans on toast when we stopped further out on Salisbury Plain.

While Blanco kept us specialists busy with the technical side of gunnery the Command Post signaller, a smiling lad called Charlie, specialised in seducing the housemaid at each large farm we stopped at. His erotic tales often passed the time as we waited with Blanco or his assistant Rumble for the next order to move.

We were at Dovercourt, outside Harwich, with the guns parked and ready to defend the submarine base on the Stour when Blanco suddenly breezed into the temporary Command Post, with the news that the Major was to have a permanent assistant, the BC/ac, who was to take over a new Bren Carrier arriving that afternoon. He insisted that I had volunteered for the job and

72

would have to go on a 200 mile convoy at 09.00hrs the next day.

No-one in the Battery had ever driven a tracked vehicle before and so with his typical enthusiasm he said we would both give it a try. The Carrier Universal - 4 tons, with a Ford V8 Engine still smelling of hot paint and oil - and a load of instruction books and record charts was unloaded from a trailer by the Ordnance Corps. Blanco got me to sign for it and then for the next two hours we took it in turns to try it out in a rough field that had apparently been used for quarrying. It got

'Oscar'

so hot that one of us at a time cooled down by sitting on the grass. I was left to 'perfect' my technique before topping up the fuel from the Battery fuel bowser ready for the morning.

I left it in the 'wagon lines' over night and kept the distributor arm in my pocket. Blanco knew that I was delighted and, apparently our Major, Oscar, had approved. Having my own vehicle would open up great new possibilities - especially as it would carry the 'X' sign of a Major. I awoke before reveille next morning and tried the engine. I regarded it as a sort of Christmas present - my very own vehicle.

Perhaps luckily I had no time to worry about the War - it was going badly. Hitler had begun to sweep across Russia from June 22nd; the battle of the Atlantic was getting worse for our shipping and only the British mainland seemed safe from invasion - Hitler was just too busy elsewhere.

But then a lowly soldier could do nothing about the position - only just do his job as well as he could. There seemed little object in being miserable. In fact I was enjoying the challenge and excitement of my life. We now had real leaders, in Blanco and Rumble, who seemed to share my views.

I also got on well with Oscar, who joined in my interest in wildlife. He never complained at my behaviour but would just give me clear orders with a grin. He insisted that I learn to drive every vehicle in the Battery and let me take a motorcycle for two days and teach myself to ride. He never even asked where I went but suggested I start by riding in some nearby woodland.

73

CHAPTER TWELVE

THE BREN CARRIER

The next morning Oscar told me that I was to drive by myself as the last vehicle in a Battery convoy exercise. I had two problems. Although the head of the convoy may move at a steady pace the end of the convoy would be moving in bursts of high speed and I had not driven the Carrier on tarmac roads. The two dispatch riders would, he said, see I did not get lost as I could not drive and follow a map at the same time - even if I had been told the route.

As I anticipated, the head of the convoy moved steadily away but when my turn came I soon got up the speed to thirty mph. But at the first

corner I realised too late that the metal tracks had little sideways grip on roads, and so I sailed across the pavement through a low wooded fence into a herbaceous border.

As an angry lady appeared from the house I engaged reverse and backed on to the road and was soon tearing away as the last vehicle disappeared from sight. I managed to keep up without collision, as there was so little civilian traffic about. I found a Carrier Universal tremendous fun to drive, although sharp bends in the road had to be skidded around, by engaging a low gear.

Soon each of the three Troop Captains also got their own carriers with a regular OP assistant each. In a few days we were engaging in cross-country races and, despite its being strictly frowned upon, we all did 'road spinning'. This entailed going down a steep hill at full speed and suddenly locking one track. The carrier would then spin up to three revolutions before - if we were lucky - carrying on in the original direction. The Army tried to counter this by making us mend our own tracks from the spares we always carried. Our Officers only became passengers if they had no other means of travel. I often carried the wireless signaller in the back and we would get called back to pull out other vehicles who were stuck in the mud. The carrier later was used to charge snowdrifts to clear the roads.

I learned to keep some slight fault on the braking system so that I always had a chit in my pocket from our Staff Sergeant artificer to say that the carrier was 'being road tested after repair.'

The casualty rate among the specialists increased and I found myself almost continually on manoeuvres, often coming back with one lot and being stopped at the gate to turn around to join the next lot out.

'Colonel'

I loved the life as the Officers were very kind to me, with no questions asked where I went in the evenings. I usually took my Carrier to a shop each day to get a daily paper.

My farm upbringing had given me the toughness to enjoy the gypsy life. I often shaved in a stream at dawn and slept in farm buildings, high up under a Dutch barn or under a hedge beside my Carrier. I loved mingling with foxes and badgers at night. As the Battery Commander's assistant I always had an excuse not to be on any parade or inspection. As I was rarely on a Pay Parade I got the Army to put half my pay into a Post Office account so that I could stop at a Post Office if I needed money.

At the end of manoeuvres I was usually given permission to break convoy back to base and get back in my own time. Using the X sign of a Major's vehicle I would gather up a few pals and do a round of public baths, café meals, a cinema and a public house before getting back to base overnight. I carried a set of maps and luck was with us.

I found it very exciting at an O.P. when the guns were firing and the shells could be heard shuffling in the sky over our heads. Oscar was very interested in bird-watching and we would search the sky with our binoculars; once we stopped firing as we saw buzzards near the target area. When I was not required at the O.P. I could always join the others at the Command Post. I was happy as both Oscar and Blanco never complained about my behaviour, and I, in turn, never gave any trouble although I often bought my own food and was very tired at times. I could sleep anywhere I found myself free. I realised that at any moment the Battery could go into barracks or operate on a Troop basis so that my services would not be needed and I would again be liable to parades, guard duties and marching drill. We were still not rated as tradesmen.

Fully armed!

We were doing mobile coast protection work in Norfolk when an extra large notice appeared on the board. It was headed RADIOLOCATION. Volunteers were required from men who were of rank lance sergeant and below, British subjects, A1 Medical grade, with school certificate standard in maths, physics and English. A personal recommendation by the commanding Officer was also required as to character. No previous knowledge required.

I went into the Battery Office and got the application form from the Postings Clerk. He told me he had posted himself to his home town three times since his call-up, and he suggested I fill up the form taking a rather imaginative view of my formal education. This I did and was called in by Major Oscar the next day who pointed out the advantages of staying with the West Somerset Yeomanry, and that I had every opportunity for promotion if I required it. He said he could not refuse to recommend me if I wished. The Officers seemed even more considerate after that; I was even told of a new racket to get an extra day's leave by Blanco's No 2, Mr Rumble.

As the autumn and winter of 1941 set in, I had a full set of oilskins for my driving and enjoyed an exciting journey to the Welsh Black Mountains for firing guns. We did have several exercises to test endurance: the Army once tried to keep the Officers and Command Post staff awake for a week. We moved the position of guns constantly so that we could never rest. In the end we all had very red eyes and could not walk straight. Several collided with obstacles and tripped up. Only the drivers were spared and I did not take my Carrier. It was the Officers who first cracked.

During that winter we rarely stayed long in one place. Tilshead on Salisbury Plain, Southminster towards the Essex Marshes and manoeuvres in the rural Midlands. The convoys were often enlivened by the lorries deliberately running down poultry and small piglets in the roads. These would later feature in the rations. On long journeys drivers were becoming sleepy: on one Divisional Exercise a notice said that 19 civilians had been killed on the road, most of them after dark.

On one exercise I was second vehicle and following the lighted rear axle of the vehicle in front had gone around the back of the pumps at a petrol station. I later learnt that all the rest followed and that the Quad gun-tractors with their ammunition limbers and guns in tow had finally flattened the site. Luckily each driver seemed to think he was the first to deviate.

One of the great horrors of lengthy manoeuvres was the Army Mobile Shower which was I considered a form of torture. The RASC operated a lorry with a large tank of water aboard. There were two outlet pipes leading to a lengthy pipe with holes all along its length. On one outlet pipe a small grinning little soldier played a large blow lamp, so that warm water in theory would flow from the long pipe.

Postings Clerk

The idea was for the men to remove their clothes at one end and walk slowly the length of the pipe soaping themselves as they went. The system however seemed completely uncontrollable and was alternately scalding or freezing so that the men emerged as red, white and blue as the Union Jack. I usually managed to find a town with public baths and leave my Carrier outside complete with its 'X' code sign.

In January we were at Tillingham near the Essex coast. I was the only O.P. assistant with a carrier available for Forward Officer manoeuvres with the Somerset Light Infantry near Billericay. For ten days our Captains would take it in turns to pretend we had guns firing over the infantry as they 'fought' over a battle course. I would return to a bed space reserved for me in a hut each evening after dark. I was then free until the next day when I would go to the Officers' billet to pick up a new Captain. I gathered that as my maps were marked they knew exactly what was coming but made no effort to get a relief Carrier, it being a rule that no one was to drive another man's vehicle.

When I returned on the night of 30 January 1942 one of my fellow O.P. assistants was waiting for me with a fifteen-cwt Battery truck. He said I was to return at once to Tillinghan for posting early the next morning. It was urgent, as he believed I was to go to the south coast. I quickly said good-bye to our Captain and just let him take over my Carrier and the rations - eggs, tins of beans and potatoes - in the ammunition boxes. I also had to give him my maps.

It was a nice crisp winter's night as I set out, without maps, for Tillingham some forty miles away. I still had my prismatic compass and tried to drive due east. I had only done this full journey once, the other way, in daylight. The truck had hooded headlights, the roads were twisting and there were no markings. I drove slowly as the verges were soft and there was no moon.

I must have missed a turning as I landed up in a seaside town. I stopped by the sea and a passer-by confirmed that it was Burnham-on-Crouch. I found I was not thinking clearly as I was worried. Had they finally decided to post me as a possible trouble maker? Had the Military Police complained about a stray Bren Carrier being seen behind the odd cinema at night? Was I going to replace battle casualties in the Middle East? Why was I so suddenly taken off manoeuvres after a total of nearly three years with my local Unit?

The camp at Tillingham was right out on a marsh road. I got back just after lights out - there was no electricity. I had an Army torch and after I put the vehicle in the 'wagon lines' I found the HQ. men's hut where I had left my kit bag and three blankets in a corner. I dozed a little on the floor and after a quick early breakfast found the postings clerk.

It was a War-Office posting to a RAOC Technical Training Unit at an address in Bournemouth. I was to be released immediately. With all my kit and a suitcase I was rushed to Southminster to catch an early train. I had no time to say good-bye to anyone. I was truly one of General's casualties.

It was while examining my documents as I sat in the rail carriage that I realised I was not due to report to Bournemouth for three days. So, having caught the Exeter train out of Waterloo I spend nearly two days at home.

I had guessed it was the result of my application to go on Radiolocation so my worries were over. I soon resumed being the farm rabbit catcher but now used a shotgun. It was luxury to again sleep in a proper bed.

Farewell

79

CHAPTER THIRTEEN
COLLEGE DAYS

By the end of three days I had recovered from the sudden shock of being posted, for posting meant uncertainty. Although I was 'in' the Wartime Army, I reckoned I was never 'of' it. My soul was still back on the farm where I so quickly shed my uniform and did some useful work.

With all my kit I had now boarded the train at Crewkerne Station - to change at Templecombe for the very slow train to Bournemouth. I was a simple gunner, alone and on the move to a new Corps, the 28th (Southampton) Technical Training Unit, RAOC, known affectionately as the 'Audience' Corps, as they dished out the weaponry and sat around to watch others do the fighting. I now at least had the great satisfaction of knowing that I had left at my own request. I was still much in control of my own destiny; I had not, I hoped, joined the Army rabbits.

I pounced on a taxi at Bournemouth West station, before the driver could pretend he had another civilian fare. Taxi drivers disliked 'common' soldiers who were heavy with kit and light on a tip. He took me into a Bournemouth backstreet where I found the RAOC in part of an empty house. The Unit consisted of two elderly sergeants, visibly far past their prime, and a Captain who actually greeted me with a smile. Perhaps I was, at that time of the morning, the only man under his command. Perhaps Radiolocation had not proved too popular? Perhaps others had not filled in the application form with my poetic licence? Or, as one Yeomanry colleague had suggested 'They bloody radio waves don't 'arf play havoc with yer bollocks'.

The College clock

Here I was given an address of my private billet, and told that after a rollcall outside the Bournemouth Municipal College at 15.00hrs I was to become an Army Student, under the control of the Principal, for the next four months. Catching a trolleybus I made my way to another backstreet to be greeted by a lively little grey-haired lady. She showed me to my room, containing four beds, and invited me to join her over a cup of tea by the fire. She was eager to explain that the front sitting room was to be used by us for meals and quiet study. She also introduced me to her two grown-up daughters who seemed to be as scant of clothes as they were high on affection. They obviously had not been warned about soldiers.

At this stage there was a plop of a kitbag dropped at the front door and a few muffled curses. Promptly rescued by 'reception' my new colleague was ushered up the stairs and then joined our tea party. He was another Sid and seemed better informed about the posting as he said he was the Coastal Battery Postings Clerk. He had completed the posting himself. He wore two stripes, gained - he told us - for rescuing his inebriated Battery commander from a thicket late on a cold winter's night.

Our next caller was from the Highland Light Infantry, complete with tam-o'-shanter, and was a little bewildered to find himself in Bournemouth. Our fourth member turned out to be a lance sergeant from the Royal Engineers who lacked any physical evidence of having ever done any heavy engineering. He said he was to do with stores and later confided how he had ordered a lorry load of ATS sanitary towels for his all-male Unit as a 'parting gift'. I sensed that I was to be amongst friends.

Our first dinner in the billet was voted fair on content but high on service. We were soon exploring the delights of Bournemouth - so far unscathed by War and unsullied by other Army Units.

At just before 15.00hrs we mingled with the strange group of some fifty soldiery gathered outside the Municipal College at the Landsdowne. They were a strange sight - about half N.C.O.s with no two apparently from the same Unit. Shoulder flashes indicated RA, RASC, RAC, RAOC, and a variety of Infantry Regiments from a variety of counties - even the Scots Highland Division. There were even two wearing the blue of the RAF. I wore my better battledress with the blue and red of the RA and Drake's Drum of the 45th Wessex Division.

One sergeant from the office was there to get us into some sort of lines before we were dismissed to file into the lecture theatre. I bet they could never have got this lot to do any drills for obviously most had not been on a parade for months. I was even beginning to get an inferiority complex.

Our first speaker was the Captain, an elderly colonial type who drew an analogy between the joys of his own early life as a gold prospector and our opportunity to learn a new trade at the very frontiers of science. We would be on probation for three weeks and 'anyone feeling unable or unwilling to go on with the course would be placed on the 'Y' list'. This was, we all knew, the pool of men used to replace battle casualties. I expect we all knew that 'Willy D' (the War Department) did not like failed volunteers.

There would, he said, be a small Army notice board in the foyer - where I already imagined 'Chad' would soon be depicted peering over a wall and all notices would be attributed to 'Confucius He Say'. He bid us all to take full advantage of the cultural and recreational facilities of Bournemouth and quickly left the scene.

The Principal, a rather mild-speaking man, was left to gently fire the big guns. He was sure that most of us had almost forgotten our School Certificate work. So the Army, in their great kindness, would give us three weeks to reach that standard again. A written examination - with a 60% pass mark - would confirm our desire to finish the course. After that exams would be weekly with a final examination at the end. Failure of an examination for any reason, including illness, could lead to instant expulsion.

The classes would be from 09.00hrs to 22.00hrs at night in three four-hour periods. We would attend morning and evening one day and just the afternoon the next day. Every other weekend would be from late Friday night until Monday afternoon when we could apply to go home. We were divided into classes of twelve with hour-long alternating sessions of theory and practical. Apparently the Army had already been draining off those with experience of electrical and wireless. So I immediately formed the conclusion that the new Army students were the loners and misfits from the military machine. We would all start from the beginning. Luckily my experience with Artillery Survey seemed to have covered much of the maths requirement. But I bought a book in Bournemouth that covered the School Certificate syllabus.

Our class tutor was an older kindly schoolmaster, with straggly hair, who seemed delighted to find pupils so keen to learn. He was assisted by an ex-infant school teacher, wearing sergeant's stripes, who articulated every word he said to us. He would always pronounce his 'g's as 'k's. Thus he would greet us with an enthusiastic 'good mornink'. To which, after a few days practice, we would chorus back 'good mornink - mein Herr!' We occasionally were to join another class for a more formal lecture by a wireless expert: a younger man who finally turned up dressed as an Officer.

After two days I felt confident to tell my tutors that I had not in fact got any school certificate and they assured me that everything necessary for our exams would be shown to us. I had nothing to worry about. In fact the atmosphere was such that we all were swept along - it seemed almost too easy. We took notes in our exercise books and I found I could tidy them up in about an hour a day back at our billet.

It was here that we had our first problem. After three days we found that our room was not being dusted or cleaned properly. There seemed to be great night activity in our house and next door. The two daughters failed to get our meals on time.

The climax came when we arose for our breakfast and Sid called us to the window to look out on the back yard of the next-door house. To our horror we could see that a couple of kennels in the yard were not occupied by dogs but human babies who were crawling around on the concrete. My colleagues, who seemed more knowledgeable that me, agreed that we were living in a brothel. It took the Army about an hour to send a doctor to inspect the billet and get us moved to a far superior billet near Bournemouth's central station and a two-minute trolley-bus ride to the College.

I soon fully adapted to this new Army way of life. We never acted as a unit so I joined three others to play tennis at Boscombe courts, on free afternoons. I ran down to the swimming baths, by the central pier, wearing only shorts and singlet for a daily swim with another student. Sid, from my billet, used to join on Sunday afternoons for the classical music concert at the Winter Gardens. I joined another group to play chess. There was a WVS canteen and reading rooms across the road from the College at the Landsdowne.

I went to the cinema at least once a week (the usherettes would let us have the best seats for 6d), and there was the Repertory theatre. The War seemed not to exist - except when a couple of bombs were dropped one night in the duck pond in the lower gardens, another damaged the Anglo Swiss Hotel and a third landed at the Central station. A piece of railway truck lodged in the garden outside the window where our dear landlady was cooking our dinner. Bournemouth was said to be an 'open' town without defences; it did act as a staging post for hundreds of RAF Aircrew.

After the first exam at three weeks, when only two students 'disappeared', the studies became increasingly interesting. We had ten special circuits to construct and study in great detail. We used Cathode Ray Oscilloscopes and sensitive meters for measurements.

We learnt how to make our own wireless sets using valves, condensers, resistors, capacitors and transformers. The whole exercise became a great game and I found I had become addicted to playing with the equipment. The Special circuits had names like Kip Relay, Squegging Oscillator, Puckle Time Base, Super Heterodyne Receiver, Negative Feedback Circuit and - my own favourite, the Multivibrator.

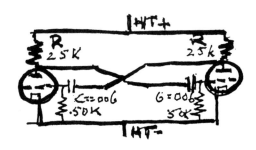

Multivibrator

Nothing we learnt was secret and Radiolocation was a distant reward for passing the course. We were never told where we would have to go or how the special circuits would be used. We would be individually posted.

In the blazing hot summer of 1942 we all became deeply bronzed and as we neared the final period it was announced that we would stay at the College for a further month for workshop practice. So after the final examination was safely passed we said farewell to our theory tutors and came under the spell of a couple of rather surly civilian craftsmen.

It was at this late stage that I saw my first 'War' casualties - most of my fellow students seemed to have never used their hands for practical purposes. The hacksaw, the metal drill, the file, the tin-snips and even the soldering iron had nasty habits of assaulting human flesh. It was perhaps fortunate that we were not allowed to use power tools.

At the end of each early session the First Aid box was raided, the blood wiped from toolbench and vice - and even the floor -and the wounded 'warriors' would disperse to their various billets. The worst injuries were caused by hacksaw blades breaking at unsuspecting moments or when hot solder or resin splashed on to skin.

War wounded!!

It was mid-July when our glorious summer holiday came to an end. And, late in the evening we dispersed out of Bournemouth stations to a delayed home leave and to await the next stage of our training for the coveted 'red sparks' - already known as the 'flying ass'ole'.

CHAPTER FOURTEEN
RADIO SCHOOL NORTH BERWICK

At home I soon reverted to farming and the catching of rabbits. The time of the year was between haymaking and harvest: a total relaxation for me from the exhilaration of College life.

After a week my orders arrived. I was to report to a Radio Maintenance Section of the Ordnance Corps with an address at a barracks in Edinburgh.

As my rail warrant did not specify a route I decided to go via London and catch the Scotsman out of Kings Cross Station. I stayed at the Red Shield Club near Euston Station overnight. The blitz bombing had been a bit patchy, I thought, and I saw the crowds who still slept in the Underground at night. Old men offered to carry my baggage for the price of a cup of tea. I had thought that private soldiers were the poorest paid in the land. I was mighty glad to leave.

I took a taxi in Edinburgh which dumped me and all my kit at the entrance of a large barracks. The guard told me the RAOC inhabited a caged building at the far side of the immense square. It was called the Hen Coop.

As I sat on my kit bag contemplating my next move I was joined by a fellow sufferer who said he had also been at Bournemouth. He frowned on my suggestion that we walk around the sacred barrack square. It was, I knew, an offence to 'defile' the square by walking across it. We sat a while as he told me of his rather dangerous hobby: he 'collected' Sergeant Majors. He wanted to see the hugely savage specimen who, we agreed, must - like a dragon - defend this square.

We set out, hatless and overladen, across the centre. We almost reached the far side when a terrific roar went up - with a distinctly Scots accent. We pretended not to hear. As we reached the far side we were confronted by a pair of very shiny boots overlaid by Scots 'trews' and a sleeve bearing the sign of a real Sergeant Major. We both dropped our baggage around us in an untidy heap and looked up - slowly.

Recruits Sir!!

He was a truly magnificent specimen in full fury, slightly trembling as he stood rigidly to attention. I left my colleague to explain that we were new Army recruits from the South of England looking to join the 'Audience' Corps. His disdain for both the Sassanachs and the Audience Corps must have been such that he thought it beneath his dignity to even properly reprimand us. With a cry of "Uuuch" he waved us on and into the Hen Coop. My pal, who said he suffered from the name of Claude, seemed mighty pleased with this Scots specimen: he just muttered "Magnificent!"

Inside the Hen Coop our documents were carefully checked and we were given a new plastic hat badge and RAOC shoulder flashes before being welcomed by a Radio Staff Sergeant.

We were then directed to join four other students and their kit who had arrived earlier. They sat at a table in the annex of the Radio Workshop. There were notices on the inner door giving restricted entry only to qualified mechanics. There was a row of boots outside which reminded me of an eastern temple.

Holy places

Soon our Staff Sergeant joined us to explain that we were not allowed to enter the Shop but would have to study our books - or even read the papers - in the annex. We would not be allowed to enter a Radio (Radar) set but could - if he could arrange it - travel out to gunsites to help carry heavy repair or calibration equipment. Claude reckoned we were not 'fish, flesh or fowl' and were at this stage the most useless people in the whole Forces. We did visit sites and actually see Radar sets for the first time.

The Radio School was some twenty miles away at North Berwick and we would have to wait until there were vacancies in the classes being made up each week for the four week Radio Mechanics qualifying course. We would have to sleep in a vacant house a mile distant but all our meals would be provided in the vast cookhouse of the adjoining barracks. We would be free after 17.00hrs on weekdays with free weekends.

Thus I was able, mostly with Claude, to sample the delights of Edinburgh for two weeks before we both were directed to take the train to North Berwick via Drem. A lorry met us at the station and dumped us beyond the barbed wire that surrounded the Marine Hotel. Blue Cap military police examined our documents and coded our AB64 identification books. I found it rather daunting - as if we were going to prison.

Having dumped our kit - four to a room - on the fourth floor we were directed to a classroom with desks on each of which was placed a copy of the 'OFFICIAL SECRETS ACT part 2' for us to read and sign. We were then given a stern warning about absolute security.

Marine Hotel - North Berwick

No documents or discussions about Radio were to take place outside a locked classroom or outside a Radio Set in the garden. We must not talk radio even at meal times or in the bedrooms as the ATS girls doing all the domestic work and cooking had not been sworn to secrecy. Our books would be kept in a locked safe inside the classroom. The Army had spies around the town to check security: they had even been known to work as bar-maids. Failure to observe these rules would lead to instant dismissal and even a prison sentence.

We had now joined the 'brethren'. Our two Staff Sergeant tutors joined us for a pep talk. There were twelve of us for the new class and it was plainly evident that the method of teaching was to be through kindness, enthusiasm and a carrot at the end. Those gaining a high mark would qualify for more courses. Apart from day classes we could do extra study for two hours - 20-22 hrs - in a special locked classroom if we wished. There was a final command to 'enjoy the course'. There would be no military training and we must try to keep ourselves fit.

The next morning the twelve of us, wearing overalls and plimsolls, assembled outside a barred and locked door on the ground floor. Above us a notice read

'BEWARE HIGH VOLTAGES. MEN CAN BE REPLACED BUT EQUIPMENT IS SCARCE'. Our Staff Sergeant tutor, bubbling with jollity and enthusiasm, joined us and the door was opened so that we could file inside to be seated at individual tables. The door was again locked. The windows were frosted and curtained. From a safe we were each handed a personal notebook and a set of circuit diagrams.

It was a strange feeling of being quite willingly trapped, the outside world ceased to exist, and my mind was totally concentrated on what we were being told. It was a bit like caving - we were searching for the secrets of Radar.

Then along the front wall an enormous circuit map was let down like a large roller blind. It was the complete 250-valve circuit diagram of the Radar GL Mark 1* Receiver. It looked like a road map of London.

"Within your first week you will know every wire, valve and component in this Receiver", announced our Tutor.

I must have involuntarily shaken my head for, in truth, six months ago I hardly knew the difference between AC and DC.

"That goes for all of you," he added, "otherwise you would not be here!"

With the aid of 'block schematic diagrams' and our knowledge of the 'special circuits' learnt from College the complexities of the Sets began to fall into place. It was as exhilarating as it was exhausting. Classes were for only forty five minutes without a break.

There were a number of these secret locked rooms, each with different equipment. Most had exposed circuitry with round green eyes and masses of glowing valves. Some, like the VT98, stood nearly three feet high and had special cooling radiators incorporated in their heads. There were masses of colour coded components, some housed in oil baths.

Voltages, up to 60K, flowed along the wires and we could pick sparks from the buttons of our overalls. We were able to monitor the voltages and examine the wave forms that flowed through the circuits.

After the first week we were introduced to the 'Fault Finding' rooms. Here the entire set circuitry was housed on a shelf running around the room. Underneath the shelf the components were connected by insulated connector pins. We took it in turns to turn our backs while the tutor removed a pin while the circuit was switched off.

The 'victim' would be allowed two minutes to switch the set on, find the 'fault' and explain to the class what was wrong - all without getting electrocuted or damaging the components. This exercise confirmed our addiction to Radar.

We had three Marks of Gun Laying Radars to study as well as the SLC Radar fixed to searchlights - and used in the Beaufighter by the RAF. We also had to study Army diesel generators, wireless sets, telephones, Tannoy loud hailers and battery-charging equipment. The method was first theory, then taking the item to bits and finally re-assembling it and testing.

Although we were free to leave the hotel if we wished outside class times, we tended to study most evenings and just managed a quick walk to the nearest pub for an evening half pint. We kept our beds down and often slept for a few precious minutes in the day. I had hoped climbing stairs would keep me fit.

From first entering the door we were shown great kindness by everyone and this after a few days caused a rumour. Could it be that the radio waves would indeed kill or sterilise us over a period? Was the consideration given us because we were about to suffer a worse fate than death? One of our number reckoned that we would each be asked for our last wish.

When we mentioned this to our tutor we learnt the full story. There was thought to be a possibility - not backed by medical science - that Radar waves would cause infertility. Many of the men who had been on radio for some time, and most were married, had put it to the test. The result was that the world was gradually being populated by the 'sons and daughters of Radar'.

The next rumour was that as we all had been so badly demilitarised and that Radio Officers had so little military training we were to be issued with a distinctive blue uniform. Within a week it was announced that all the Army's repair people were to be used to form a new Corps: The Royal Electrical and Mechanical Engineers (otherwise known as 'Ruin Every Make of Equipment!').

So we were once again dished out new plastic hat badges and shoulder flashes. The rank of 'Craftsman' would replace 'Private' for tradesmen.

My only worry now was not to lose control of my fate when the course ended. I would need to get the 80% in the final examination. Otherwise I might be posted abroad ...

There was, we were told, another Radio School near Cairo.

The restrictions put on our studying time made swotting difficult - taking documents out of the classroom would be far too risky. So I found another member of the class, with similar views, who would share my Mark 2 Swotting scheme.

Working in a closed classroom with sparks a-flying and valves a-flashing could be very hot so we usually wore our overalls over our running shorts. Thus it was quite easy to write in pencil upon our persons. Tiny bits of circuitry, formulas, and sequences could, after work each fine day, be taken for a run over the golf course adjoining the hotel and for a run along the deserted beach up

"That's the control valve just past my navel!"

towards Tantalon Castle.

Having got hot and panting we could sit by the sea and revise the tricky bits of the course - suitable for examination test papers. As a final gesture we would dive into the waves to remove the marks before returning to the hotel to relax in both body and mind. It seemed to work and I was called out of class for 'sentence'.

Three days before we left our senior class student was called to the office and given a poster requesting volunteers for service on the Anti-Aircraft guns and searchlights around the Naval Base at Scapa Flow in the Orkneys.

The posting would rank as 'overseas', thus meriting double leave, free cigarettes, extra rations and clothing and cheaper supplies at the NAAFI. It would be a six month posting with an option to remain. It was particularly recommended for rural type soldiers with an interest in nature study. Those volunteering would collect any outstanding leave directly after this course.

My name was the first on the list and I was once again back in Somerset trying to explain to the locals the strange ways of modern warfare.

CHAPTER FIFTEEN
JOURNEY TO THE MAGNETIC NORTH

Long train journeys during Wartime were pretty grim. The normal necessities of eating, sleeping, washing or just resting were restricted and uncertain. The station names were taken away and the carriages and stations were very dimly lit at night. Timings were uncertain and connections could so easily be missed. Often full kit had to be carried and looking after all the bits and pieces - and getting them off and on during changes - was as demanding as a hen minding her chickens in a thicket.

There was also the difficulty of conversing with fellow sufferers. All information about troop numbers, movements or disposition of Units was secret, so conversation with strange servicemen -the girls travelled first class with the Officers - was best restricted to bursts of invective about the conditions of travel. Those of us joining a Unit after a secret course had to be extra careful. There were spies about from both sides.

I had met two students at Radio school who found a solution to the problem when travelling together. They put the word 'UG' before every vowel. So that 'I am posted to a new unit' would become 'UGI UGAM PUGOSTUGED TUGO NUGEW UGUNUGIT'. Practice had made them so efficient that once, when they were waiting at a bus stop, a kindly elderly lady had asked them in for a cup of tea. She had thought that they were 'gallant foreign troops' from a place called UGENGLUGAND in deep Eastern Europe. They also wore their hats back to front so no one could see the badges. They showed me how they could alter the inserted two letters - say from UG to EK - to throw off eavesdroppers.

93

I started off at the little station of Chard in deep Somerset and fourteen hours later I booked in at the Rail Transport Office at Perth in Scotland. Here the military trains, politely called Jellicoes, would take me on to Thurso - and the boat. I was grimy, tired, feeling like an Army rabbit and realising that I had, as yet, done less that half of my journey.

I did manage to meet two of my recent student pals from North Berwick and dumping our kit behind the barrier ventured out in the darkened streets to find a fish and chip shop and get a wash and brush up.

We arrived back in time to get seats together - the train was full. The other five in the compartment seemed delighted to tell us of the horrors that the journey might hold for us. The train would be nine hours slowly winding its way up through the Highlands - unless snow was blocking the line in the Grampians. Men had been known to die before being rescued, so they said. When we finished with the train the boat journey across the Pentland Firth could even mean that some would reach their final destination by ambulance. It would seem that in really bad weather "Death would be a kind relief, mate," as one sailor put it.

We three agreed that after the last happy eight months a bit of penance would not, perhaps, harm our military souls. So we just became resigned to our fate. The compartment did become hot, stuffy and tainted. In periods of depression men snored, belched and farted with great abandon. I spent frequent short periods battling with the extra kit in the corridor and gazing out of the windows.

We stopped at Dingwall to take on a second engine. After Inverness the mountains could be seen with flocks of red deer quite close to the line, even inside the snow barriers. Even at night it was most impressive with a clear starlit sky. There were glimpses of the sea and of the two struggling engines and leading carriages as the single track slowly wound its way northwards.

After what someone said was Hemsdale, the slow train came to a stop. With cries of 'Perth next stop!' it started going backwards before resuming its journey inland across the more desolate part of Caithness to finally arrive at Thurso just before dawn.

Here we were herded into the Transit Camp where we could rest in Nissen huts and have a substantial fatty breakfast of sausages, eggs and mash. From the experienced travellers - mostly Navy or Airforce - we soon learned of the 'delights' of the boat trip awaiting us.

The Camp overlooked the swirling waters of the Pentland Firth and the sea was flecked with 'white horses' as the waves shattered in the wind. We learnt that the Stromness boat, the Earl of Zetland (only 548tons), had a particularly evil reputation. It had been built for inter-island work in the Shetlands and bobbed around like a cork. It was, as one sailor remarked, 'torpedo proof' as so little of it was below the water line.

After breakfast I just had time to look around the Camp to see if there was a back exit if I was ever stuck there. It was announced that the first boat would be the Zetland and a lorry would take our kitbags to the dock.

Then in the dim light of dawn a group of us gathered in the road. With a couple of sergeants circling us like Highland sheep dogs we 'marched' erratically down the road towards the port area. The Earl of Zetland could be seen bobbing towards the pier.

After a check of documents we filed out on to the jetty and on to the Zetland. The wind was beginning to rise and we sat surrounded by our kit on deck. A few went down into the hold - probably designed for holding cattle. The few Officers and Wrens filed into the cabins.

It was my first experience of a small sea-going boat and I clung to a bollard up towards the front. Within ten minutes the Zetland started rocking. So I joined a few others at the rail and, as if I had swallowed some red hot coals, I bid good-bye to my breakfast.

The movement became more violent and we were all ordered into the hold just as waves started to rise over the bow and hit the bridge. The hold hatches were closed; inside we all had gathered our kit to sit on to be retained with our legs as we held on for dear life to the surrounding framework.

The ship seemed to roll and pitch even more violently, as each time she would dip into the waves gallons of water started coming down from a gap in the centre of the roof. This did have the effect of washing the floor but gradually odd items of kit joined the wash and rolling kit bags were adding to the hazard. It seemed that the propeller must have been threshing thin air at times for the forward motion would spasmodically cease in the bow-down position.

Finally there was a crack and a piece of framework came away; two bodies joined the scurrying debris. It was impossible to give them assistance as

The old bugger's smiling!

they seemed to have given up trying to help themselves. Then as they slithered around a small hatch opened at floor level and an arm grabbed them both and they disappeared out of sight.

After a very long hour the motion damped down and the hatch cover was opened. I struggled up on deck. To our starboard were high cliffs with the unmistakable sight of the Old Man of Hoy - a high stack rising out of the sea with the general shape of a human face on high. I remember thinking that he was smiling.

Further on, a waterfall was coming over the top of the thousand-foot vertical red cliffs at St John's Head - the water never reached the sea but was blowing back over the top. Seagulls of many species circled the boat. There were skuas, guillemots, razor-bills and hundreds of puffins.

Even with a greatcoat I was feeling shivery, but the fresh salt air was untainted by humans. The Island scenery before us was low, grey and treeless as we turned into Hoy Sound and then made for the small collection of buildings and huts that was Stromness.

At the far end of the jetty were a group of lorries. The drivers in oilskins, balaclavas and mittens waved an arm towards the lorry requested. About ten men scrambled into the Caldale Vehicle with its new REME flash. For forty minutes we travelled along a metalled road through marsh and heathland, through a tiny settlement someone said was Finstown and finally turned down a track and stopped at some form of guard hut. Then on down the road we squelched into an area of black hangars, great square concrete blocks and black Nissen huts. For the information of we six new recruits to the camp someone said "This mates, is yer fucking home - Caldale."

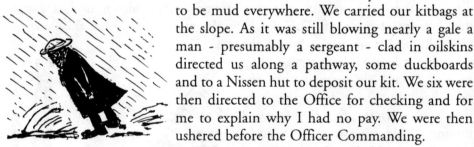

We dismounted with difficulty as there seemed to be mud everywhere. We carried our kitbags at the slope. As it was still blowing nearly a gale a man - presumably a sergeant - clad in oilskins directed us along a pathway, some duckboards and to a Nissen hut to deposit our kit. We six were then directed to the Office for checking and for me to explain why I had no pay. We were then ushered before the Officer Commanding.

He was a Major, rather shabby, wearing his hat and a jerkin over his battle dress. He was unsmiling with a north country accent. "Life int' Orkney can be grim," he counselled. "Camp is expanding so look out for water-filled trenches after dark. We've all got job to do here - so work hard. Ther's nowt much else to do. Remember - everything in these Islands is secret - nothing you hear or see must go any further - limit your letters home to hoping they are well and you hope to see them soon."

Unknown soldier in Orkney

96

That was it and he instructed the sergeant to see we all got our coupons and extra supplies.

We had a good late dinner and located the NAAFI and the nearest wash house before drawing our extra clothes and blankets, and getting our beds laid so that we could catch up on some sleep. The stove was lit in mid afternoon and so the hut became comfortably warm.

After breakfast the next morning there was some sort of roll call - but only half the names seemed to be answered. Anyone working after 18.00hrs the previous evening was exempt as were those on leave, ill, courses or presumably still fast asleep. The great moment had, we thought, arrived.

In a newer part of the Camp amid the diggings and new building was a small square with a few fully assembled Radar sets, plus a Nissen hut. This had an annex and the usual row of boots outside a door with the red sparks. Dressed in our overalls and carrying our plimsolls one of the Corporals among us boldly opened the door to announce our arrival.

After the promises about our new trade we were in for a big shock. We never even got inside the door, for the man in charge, who appeared to be a Sergeant Major, held up his hands in horror and said there was no work for us. He directed us to the Camp Office to find the Sergeant Major in charge of 'general duties'. So finding the NAAFI open we had a cup of char while we considered our fate.

The GD Sgt Major on the other hand seemed delighted to see us. He explained to us his strange theory. He said the mud that covered the Camp was due to the fact that the rain water from the roofs was all going straight into the drains. So we were put to filling sandbags and blocking the drains. At least we got to know the various 'Shops', who normally operated behind closed doors, and who did not quite appreciate having their drains blocked.

It rained very heavily that night and we were not entirely surprised that a scream went up the next morning that the depth of mud around the camp had doubled - standing at six inches outside the gun shop.

I never had an opportunity to see the Sergeant Major's brilliant next move - although I understood that fire hoses had been alerted - as I waded to breakfast with the help of duckboards. Two of us had been called into the office and told our journey north had not yet stopped. We were told to report to the RAF Unit on Shapinsay Island. They would teach us, in a week, how to handle the Mark 6 Kite Balloon, used for flying over boats to prevent dive bombing and also used to carry a small oscillator on high for Radar calibration. Sam and I were given fifteen minutes to collect some of our kit and join a lorry for Kirkwall

Pier and the drifter.

As we boarded the drifter in fine weather we were now clad in jerkins and oilskins. The little drifter lay low in the water and within twenty minutes we were tied up in the jetty by Balfour Castle. In the grounds lived two sections of RAF. One kept the fast Air Sea Rescue Launch ready for emergencies at sea. The other section of some ten men and a sergeant took the balloons to and from the freighters that gathered in Kirkwall Bay waiting to join conveys around Norway to the Russian port of Murmansk.

Life with the RAF was very relaxed. Each morning for two hours one of their number would give us theory and practice on rope work - knots and splicing - balloon fabric - repairing and securing - inflating with hydrogen and testing for purity. We then learnt about the theory of handling and bedding down on wire and picket beds.

The rest of our time we joined them in handling these 36x18ft monsters, often in high winds. Both of us REME men had a farming background, so dealing with violent creatures on the end of a rope was not entirely new to us. Each day we would go out to the ships in the drifter - laying fishing nets on the way out and pulling in on the way back. The drifter was manned by two civilians - a skipper and an engineer who took us over the works below.

During our week there was Highland dancing and an ENSA Concert Party with Richard Murdoch. As a course it was the most undemanding and we could only treat it as an extra holiday. It was during this course that I realised how glorious Island life could be. I had been able to see something of the life in the sheltered sea and to explore a tiny wind-swept forest on Shapinsay where the fully grown oak trees on the windward side were only three feet high. All too soon we were going back to Caldale.

CHAPTER SIXTEEN

THE REME WORKSHOP AT CALDALE

In the countryside of my youth there was a sort of strict pecking order amongst both creatures and humans. 'Everyone knowed 'is place', I was told. The Squire, with his mansion and estate, came at the top. Then there was a whole range of farmers and smallholders, followed by the various rural craftsmen: carpenters, blacksmiths, thatchers, farriers, even threshing machine operators and the like, who were jealously self employed. At the bottom of the pile were the farm wage labourers. These included younger sons of smaller farmers, like myself, who were normally regarded with deep critical suspicion and who were sometimes called 'Thic Young Meister bloke', when we 'made a proper snuddle' (did something silly).

Of course the Army had its two class hierarchy by rank: OFFICERS, and other ranks. But in a workshop I met another division - by trade. The hierarchy had been led by Instruments - the skilled watch makers - the Wireless mechanics and the Electricians. Then came a whole range from motor mechanics, gun fitters, welders, tinsmiths and coppersmiths, carpenters and saddlers. Each had their own shop.

Suddenly a new species of tradesman had been invented. They had none of the long apprenticed skill or pride of the older craftsmen. They came under the banner of the Flying Ass'ole - the Red Sparks of Radiolocation - and they left their boots outside their 'secret' shrine. They - like the farming sons - were regarded with deep suspicion and I can imagine the joy amongst the Caldale craftsmen when a small party of these misguided souls could be seen blocking Caldale Camp's storm drains.

99

During my week's balloon holiday with the RAF a surfeit of Radio mechanics had turned into a positive shortage. So my boots only had few companions at the entrance of the Radio 'Shrine'. The trackways and squares of the Camp were still grimed with mud - for the builders (Royal Engineers Construction Unit) were still playing mud pies and digging water-filled foundation trenches for new buildings: they looked wet, cold and sad.

Great concrete square blocks were dotted round the camp which had been, I was told, an airship base in the Great War. I had to locate the cookhouse, the NAAFI, and some of the main hangars before darkness set in, for no external lights were allowed. Small shafts of light accompanied the clank of metal as doors opened and closed. The almost constant high wind meant that all openings were to be kept closed.

There was an air of dark gloom about the camp exterior. There was no sign of bullshit or marching men. I was told we were unlikely to ever see an Officer - they were a 'lot of drunk bastards who never left the Mess.'

The Guard Hut was half way up the track to the main road. If the enemy ever took over the Camp the guard would only hear about it over the telephone later. No one seemed concerned. There was, once, boundary barbed wire but as the Camp expanded no one seemed to think about moving out the wire, so the Camp could be approached on foot from Kirkwall, two miles distant, over the heathland and marsh.

Inside the Radio Shop was a highly polished floor, and also benches with a row of stools on which mechanics sat before an array of testing equipment. A kindly Artificer Staff Sergeant initiated me into a new game - which some called the 'bran-tub'. Spares from the factory were difficult to obtain, so panels and bits of Radio equipment had to be laboriously repaired at a bench. Components from condemned sections had to be salvaged, tested and re-used. Each job was put on a card - some big, some small - and these could be drawn out from the Shop office and store. In charge of the store was, to my great delight, a grinning Claude, who had landed himself an expected cushy number.

For the next fortnight I dipped in the 'bran-tub'. Each finished job had to be inserted in an operational Set, kept in the square outside, and tested. Then counter-signed by one of the Shop staff sergeants. My most exciting job was a large box of components - valves, capacitors, coils and resistors - that just refused to work in a Set but appeared O.K. on static testing equipment. I was allowed to test them to destruction using high voltages - a one-man fireworks display. I naturally saved enough to build myself a small wireless receiver.

If a job entailed woodwork - even putting a handle on a sweeping brush - or

100

entailed brazing tin or copper it had to do the round of other shops. If a new piece of equipment was required the Radio Office would issue an indent and I had to go to a special RAOC spares hangar adjacent to the Camp and 'buy' or order a new piece.

The job was solitary: each mechanic worked on his own, spaced along the benches, with advice and checking coming from the senior staff - mostly Staff Sergeants. It was never boring. The Armament Sergeant Major in charge of the Shop, said to have come from the film industry, rejected any job not completed to 'factory standard' of workmanship.

Most men seemed to just eat and sleep outside workshop hours - although many worked late on rushed repair jobs. In the evenings I walked to the darkened streets of Kirkwall with a workshop colleague. Late at night the aurora borealis would light up the entire sky and we could see the warships in the Flow and the outline of the distant

Hibernation

islands. In the sky above there were always strange cries of geese and other seabirds. It was so peaceful.

I asked one of the Staff Sergeants if I could 'go mobile'. For the next month I joined an experienced companion each morning. Carrying our toolboxes and with other equipment draped around our necks we would set out by truck and boat across the Islands to do heavier repairs on site with the help of the resident mechanic.

We worked on the Heavy Anti Aircraft GL Marks 1, 1* and 2 although there were over a hundred SLC sets mounted on searchlights.

We would draw our job cards from Claude and he would arrange our itinerary. A 15cwt lorry took us to the pier or our first Site job. We arranged our own transport though the AA Sites after that. As boats did not sail after dark we could get stranded for the night. We stayed on a repair until it was finished or we were relieved by another team or, as the Workshop chief put it, 'you bloody well keel over from fatigue and die'. We got the message and most jobs took about half an hour.

We would call at the Gunsite; the guard would let the REME vehicle in and we would be driven near the Set. These Sets had separate transmitter and receiver with the latter sitting in the middle of a 'mat' which consisted of about two acres of perfectly flat wire netting sitting on stilts. Like Caldale the Radio

(Radar) was outside the boundary wire, which had been trampled down.

We would be met by the resident mechanic, who lived with the Set in the Radio operator's hut. Some sites gave the mechanics a hut of their own.

If the Set was still working - it worked in three shifts around the clock - he would request a stand-down. We would be allowed only a one hour maximum for the repair or modification before the Set was reported 'out of action'.

For a Radio to be out of action was considered very serious and Admiral Frazer's office at Naval H.Q. had to be informed. The Workshop would have to be told and, so I heard, even a Radio Officer had to visit a Set. The consequences for the visiting mechanics, if a good excuse was not given or if our senior considered it due to our inefficiency or fault, could mean return to workshops and the bench ... or 'posting'.

I soon learnt the layout of the Heavy AA Gun Sites. There were six sites spread out around the Flow from beyond Stromness in the west to St Mary's in the east, where the Italian POWs were building a causeway to Burray and South Ronaldsay Islands. There were four further sites on Hoy Island and its little companion of South Walls joined by a causeway. There were other isolated Radio sites without guns at Tommy Tiffy, Rackwick and Ward Hill. This looked out over the sea from high clifftop sites.

Gulls

Many of the Site mechanics were amateur naturalists or biologists who told me about the glories of the local fauna and flora. This daily travelling to sites was hard work but was a most wonderful experience for me. We had a great freedom and satisfaction. It was now clear that the life of a Radio mechanic was to be a solitary one, for although most sites had two mechanics, the second one was either on leave, a course, having a few free hours in Kirkwall or with civilian friends - or fast asleep after a night call-out. I gathered there were Radio Officers on some sights but never met one on Site repair trips.

I was told that an order had been given that men were not to be left alone in the wild conditions after there had been a couple of suicides; others had become 'very peculiar'. A notice in the Radio Shop said that each mechanic would have to sign a document saying whether the conditions were causing him trouble, either physically or mentally, every third month. It was plain that men either loved or hated Orkney.

After working on a small isolated farm this life was, to me, a wonderful way to spend a War. I could see that, as a mechanic, I could study the Natural History of the Islands in some detail. I could again resume my agricultural studies. After I had visited most of the Gun Sites I requested that I be sent out as a Site mechanic. Each day Claude kept me in touch with vacancies, and then after a fortnight I was told to collect all my kit. I was to leave Caldale and go out to the 3.7 Anti Aircraft Site along the banks of the Flow, 3 miles the other side of Kirkwall.

During our training we were told that we would work in small sections consisting of a Radio Officer, a Staff Sergeant Artificer and four mechanics. But Orkney seemed to be a law unto itself. There were Radio Officers concealed somewhere out on the gunsites- but as yet I had never seen one. The entire work on the sites was done by resident mechanics - often alone - with back-up from the workshop at Caldale.

I was taken to the Gunsite - known as M3 - by the workshop truck. It was a windy, cool day so all I knew about the driver - in oilskins and balaclava - was that he had a red tip to his nose.

I dismounted near the Set and the operator's hut, just through the other side of the boundary wire. The four 3.7inch gun barrels were pointed skywards out of the top of their concrete emplacements. The diesel electrical generator was chugging away inside a nearby Nissen hut.

I staggered to the operator's hut with all my kit and my locked toolbox. Inside were the usual mixture of those sleeping and those going out for meals or the washhouse.

The Set was very slowly revolving with its long aerial arms searching the sky. So I knew one team was on duty, sitting on their little seats watching the green eyes - or possibly (from my knowledge of the British Army) reading books!

Inside the door was a spare bed, and next to it, in loose overalls and plimsolls was the Site mechanic. He was a rather solemn distant type whose enthusiasm for military matters would be almost nil. I had met him briefly on one of my trips; he rejoiced under the name of Corporal Hogg: his friends called him Rasher.

He was engrossed with a pocket chess set.

"Do you know Queen's pawn's gambit?" he asked, barely looking up.

"Not right now," I volunteered, hoping to be told something about my duties.

"Good move," he replied, "you ought to know it." He glanced up at me to see if I was paying attention. "Here, take a seat."

Although I had played chess I did not think at that time it took precedence over my initiation as a Site mechanic; but there was plenty of time, I thought. So for the next half hour we played chess - until the noise of another lorry outside suddenly reminded Rasher that he was due back at Caldale to go on leave the next morning. He would be away at least two weeks.

From my previous excursions I knew roughly what to do - not to interfere with equipment unless it went wrong, and to avoid getting caught up in the parades and other purely artillery activities. So parking my kit I went in search of the Sergeant in charge of the Radio operators - usually said to be mild reflective souls, seeking a quiet life. I found him talking - or trying to talk - to the operator who was refuelling the Diesel.

"Is there a Radio Officer anywhere in the Camp?" I shouted.

"Aye!" he replied, "I saw him under the mat, some time ago."

"Under the mat? Was he looking for something?"

"Liverworts," came the explanation. "I think somebody said he lives on M4."

I was already beginning to see why we were expected to sign for our sanity every third month. I found myself thinking up some strange ideas: I wanted to explore the seashore and the heathland ... I would also learn to sleep to the point of hibernation. I too could search for liverworts.

Before the afternoon darkness I had found the Troop notice board, the NAAFI and the other static points of Anti- Aircraft Gun Site. I managed to get into the Set and

Liverworts (Officer Material!)

have a look at the Service and Modification Book and see what spares I had.

After tea I heard over the Tannoy that the Radio Mechanic was wanted in the Command Post with his tool kit. I found that a wire had become loose on the telephone system. I wore my battle dress jacket - undone of course - because it showed the red sparks. As I had not had to book in at the pay office I just wondered if anyone would notice that a strange man was mending the phones. I was sorely tempted to put on a German accent.

During the evening - using a couple of Radio spares - I got my own wireless going so that I could lie in bed until Vera Lynne said goodnight to all servicemen - the rabbits and the ferrets!

I vaguely remember the search teams changing over at midnight and the central stove being stoked up for the night. Then I fell asleep to the sound of high winds clanking a piece of 'galvanise' sheeting on one of the buildings across the camp.

"Oi! You the mechanic?" someone was gently shaking me.

"Um ... um ... yes ... what's wrong?" I rubbed my eyes as the only lights in the hut were the glow from the fire and the torch held by my visitor.

"Bloody receiver is off tune - it's not picking up properly."

I started to reach for my overalls and lit my own torch. "Since when?"

"T'was those silly evening buggers - your mate showed 'em how to do it."

I'd heard the story that the Radio Mk I amplifier could be retuned and hooked to a loudspeaker to pick up wireless programmes. To properly retune the banks of amplifier circuits could be tricky without declaring the Set out of action. Luckily, with the Set still turning slowly I managed to restore it until the morrow when I was entitled to ask for a fifty-minute maintenance break. As a reward I claimed a tot of rum from the cookhouse.

It only took me a few days to realise that Site Mechanic was the job for a real 'ferret'. Although I would be repairing any electrical equipment on the Site I was almost my own boss. Most days something went wrong. The telephones would get 'bronchitis', the Tannoy loudspeakers would develop a stammer. The NAAFI wireless sets would suffer from rough treatment. The battery charger would need checking as it charged the gun batteries that worked the electric shell rammers for the guns.

I was supposed to remove and check some smaller Radio valves each day and fill out a detailed maintenance sheet for the Set. But I was advised that Radio Sets should not be interfered with too much if they worked properly.

The Site also had two classical faults that would enhance the reputation of any mechanic.

First the Camp generator - after the Diesel was momentarily closed down for an oil change - completely failed to register. Several people came screaming for me. The cure was simple; just to touch the output with a torch battery and the whole thing burst into life. This I did with a flourish and an 'Abracadabra'. The other fault was a total failure of the amplification circuits on the Radio Receiver. The cure here was even simpler. After screams for help all I had to do was to remove a particular safety screen, and, using a small spanner in the manner of a wand, give a 'sharp mechanical jolt' to the housing of the crystal oscillator that was the heart of the Set.

Great Skua

I met the Radio Officer after two days. We talked botany and he undertook to bring me my

105

free coupons for soap, chocolate and cigarettes each week. Also my sealed tin of free fifty Players cigarettes. He said I could get him by phoning the Officer's mess on the next Site. He would get me a relief mechanic so that I could have occasional days off duty. We usually met under the mat as Officers and men were, even in this military outpost, not expected to fraternise. He never questioned my statement that I never got paid.

The three teams of Radio operators were mostly older men - many from the building trades - of medical grade B. They had done a three week operators' course at their own school near St Mary's on the Island. They advised me of many tricks that 'Madio wrecks' could get up to. These included changing over two almost identical valves in equipment so that they could report it out of action. This could be used to take the Artillery minds off the idea of parades or inspections. I could also take the place of the Transmitter Operator for short spells as a sign of goodwill.

At this stage of the War it seemed that the enemy found it impossible to attack Scapa. The place was bristling with Warships of every sort and the mass of Radiolocation could pick up enemy planes as they took off from Scandinavian airfields. The AA Radio could pick them up from seventy miles. We rarely had alerts and, standing behind the operators, I saw one plane shot down by our fighters from Scotland at the extreme limits of the Radio screen.

Not to be denied a pit of fun, one of our planes would go up over the Flow at night and over a hundred searchlights would pick it up on command. Otherwise a plane would fly over the Flow in daylight and the Guns would fire at it 180 degrees out.

Each month the Orkney Barrage was fired. Over 100 heavy AA Guns and the entire AA weaponry of the Warships would put several cubic miles of hot shrapnel over the Fleet anchorage for one minute. The echoes would rattle around the Islands and sky for several minutes afterwards and some local wit would find a feather and announce that 'they got it!' It was unsafe to watch the Barrage in the open as 'hail' would often rattle on the Nissen huts. Some said that the Barrage was put on to ensure that at least once each month everyone was awake.

As the days lengthened in the spring and small flowers appeared on the heathland and under the mat I found life very pleasant indeed. I loved the howling winds as long as it was dry and the multitude of birds started to take up their nesting territories. I had even been 'adopted' by a large family in Kirkwall and was told not to even knock on the door but just walk in to meet them and several other stray visiting Radio mechanics.

It was a glorious morning when I got a phone call from Workshops. I was to be relieved of my duties and, after a week's leave, go back to College. This time University College Nottingham.

The lorry turned up later that morning with my relief mechanic. He had been on the Islands longer

Glaucous Gull

than I had. Before I left he asked me to sign a petition he was organising. It was to keep Joanna Southcoat's Box CLOSED. The driver was in a hurry so I could not tell him anything about the Site - not even if he knew Queen's Pawn's Gambit.

CHAPTER SEVENTEEN
BACK AT COLLEGE: NOTTINGHAM

The 24th (Nottingham) Tech. Tr. Gp. REME lurked in a back street. Ominously one closed door was labelled Sgt Major Savage MM. Another closed door had the Captain's name on it. A traditional-type sergeant frostily examined my papers and directed me to my billet in Shakespeare St, near the ornate buildings of University College.

The billet was a large boarding house occupied - in more civilised times - by players from the nearby Theatre Repertory Company. Six Radio Mechanics alternated meal time facilities with six American Servicemen - training at 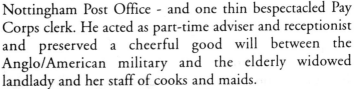 Nottingham Post Office - and one thin bespectacled Pay Corps clerk. He acted as part-time adviser and receptionist and preserved a cheerful good will between the Anglo/American military and the elderly widowed landlady and her staff of cooks and maids.

The Americans, being of French extraction, were a very expansive jolly lot. Much of their efforts were directed to sampling the delights of many of Nottingham's ten thousand surplus female workers. So that after they returned from daily study they monopolised the two bathrooms to prepare for evening battle. They had three times our pay and new uniforms so we had often to messily scramble over the scented bevy of young ladies waiting on the path and sitting on the boundary walls waiting for their amorous attentions.

The six Americans had a Colonel they called Charlie who would turn up in a Jeep to collect them for special treats.

Like Bournemouth our studies in Nottingham were non-secret. The mornings, after a rollcall in the street, consisted of lectures on valve theory and the construction of circuits. The last part consisted of rapid dictation and copying down of wave patterns, circuits and calculations which we were expected to complete in our own time in the evenings and at weekends.

We were divided into two classes of thirty each, using two college theatres and two tutors.

One of these wore sandals and had a long beard and hair like a latter-day saint. Our tutor was less woolly but both gave the impression that they were conscientious objectors and seemed to regard soldiers as an inferior species. They had to be very careful at lectures not to ask where to put anything for there was an automatic response of 'stick it up your arse!'

In contrast the afternoon periods were in workshops, specially contrived to ensure that we could not use lathes, electric drills or power saws. Here we hand-built circuits from scratch, using tin sheeting and boxes of small components and once-used electric wiring and valves. Each circuit was tested on oscilloscopes before we went on to the next. It was all quite leisurely.

We worked in ten groups of three with two tutors who never let us forget that they were the highest quality craftsmen. We had to draw all items from a central store for each circuit. They milled around us and had good reason to despise our attitude to craft work and workshop etiquette.

Unlike my stay in Bournemouth, here we met a degree of craft snobbery and the delight of the General Duty people, in the REME office, to demean the craft workers, especially the new Radio mechanics. We had our methods of reply.

We had to pass the course. The 'carrot' was that those gaining 80% in the final examination would be sentenced to go straight on to the secret Radio Maintenance School No 3. There they would study for a further advanced course on new unmentionable equipment. There were stories about this place, Gopsall Hall, that appealed to me. I had heard it was the Shangri-La of Radio.

Probably because I had done a few cartoons for the College Wall Newspaper, I was asked by two colleagues to make up a workshop group. Peter, who came from Hoy Island sub-workshop in Orkney was reputed be a classical pianist before he cut his hair and was called up. He was also reputed to be a sort of poet and thus would attract a special venom from real Sergeant Majors. He used them to prove his theory that modern man was descended from the Neanderthal cave-men. Our other member was Hugh, whom I gathered was a professional artist living in London, also a very useful character to bait the Military or top snobby craftsmen. We would, they suggested, call ourselves the Bohemians.

Hugh has been an art school teacher and during our first circuit-making session agreed to combine this with a course on Still Life. The rather expansive College workshop was well supplied with piping of all sorts and various wooden blocks used in the plumbing trade. We could, Hugh said, use sheeting to get the shadows and highlights.

So when we queued up to get our tools and supplies from the Store it was agreed that Pete and I would draw the correct kit. Hugh, on the other hand, would try to get other bits with interesting colours and textures. Hugh would explain the effect of shadows and reflected light - even daring to use a piece of blackout material to get better shade effects.

For some days our tutors seemed oblivious to the scheme, until one tutor took a wooden hammer from the still life model for us to use.

"You've destroyed the composition!" protested Hugh in an unthinking moment.

The tutor, in baffled semi-comprehension lifted up some of the other carefully arranged items. "What do you want all these for?"

"It's the reflected light," said Hugh, making sweeping gestures with his arms.

Still Life with mallet

"The only light we want around here is from your circuits!" The tutor stormed away to another group.

"The man's a cretin," said Pete, "Probably never heard of the French Impressionists."

At the beginning of the next afternoon session we had a lecture on the evils of drawing from store more equipment than we needed for one circuit. Also the correct way to ask for tools - specifying the exact size in mm. Not, as Pete did, by holding up a thumb and finger to the tutor and saying, 'A whirligig thing. About - that - size', instead of a four mm drill and bit.

The battle lines were now open and we dared another group to construct an 'infinite current circuit' to test just before closing time. Our tutors attributed the resulting fire in the main fuse box to natural causes. But they did accept the offer of three volunteers to stay behind to do some rewiring.

111

At this stage I myself felt duty bound to strike a chord for common soldiery. I had to resort to the 'exploding overalls trick'. The Army supplied three sizes of overalls which we knew as 'gigantic', 'normal' and 'dwarf'. The trick here was for two soldiers - on either side of normal - to draw clean overalls and then swap over before leaving the store.

The resulting effect was that one soldier appeared to be wrapped in a tarpaulin while the other would be trussed up like a chicken. Provided they did not stand together on a parade, only those in the know would realise what had

happened. If the latter man was asked to stand up straight and throw out his chest a well-muscled character could explode the overalls and scatter buttons far and wide.

On this occasion I was wearing 'gigantic' overalls. I had rolled up the sleeves but had tied a string below each knee like the farm workers did to keep the rats out at corn-threshing time.

When our tutor approached the Bohemians the next afternoon he, quite unnecessarily we thought, demanded to know - in loud voice - why

The overall gambit

I had my overalls hooked up. I replied, "Because of the rats."

"There are no rats in this workshop," he growled as he stormed off on his rounds. There was silence for a time.

"You can't let him get away with that!" said Hugh.

"Of course not!" echoed Pete. "If there are no rats you'll have to invent one."

So our art studies were temporarily suspended for that day while we considered a plot to redeem my veracity. After two days we put our plan in action with the help of a few chosen colleagues.

The code word to start the exercise was for me to peer into a particularly thick stack of plumbing materials stacked along the wall and shout "RATS!"

At which command a few others would join in a search and, always at the opposite end of the shop to a tutor, someone else would shout "There it goes!" As hoped, the unsuspecting tutors would be attracted to one end and we Bohemians would then take over. I was to do the kill with a resounding whack to the floor with a wooden rod. All went well.

Hugh solemnly opened the window high above the street below; Pete mimed holding a rat's tail between thumb and forefinger and swung the 'rat' out of the window.

A rather perplexed tutor just stood and said nothing. We quickly and silently resumed our job on our circuit; next morning there were no knee-strings and the overalls were returned to their rightful owners.

Rat

Our next real problem happened when Hugh was staging an exhibition of his work in a London Gallery - it was rather in the style of Manet, Monet or Renoir. He received about forty largish photographs and wanted to show us his work. Pete and I persuaded him that we must somehow stage it in the workshop. We had to think up a scheme.

The greatest bugbear with delicate Radio equipment was dust, and floors at Caldale and other REME Radio shops were kept spotless and highly polished. Although the College shop was swept at the end of work each day, we three persuaded our tutors that a really good sweep-up, especially after the rat hunt should be done during the last half hour on one day.

So the Bohemians were armed with three brooms and dustpans and we started our sweep even before the rest had cleared the workshop. The benches were against the walls and so we dusted the tops first.

As soon as both tutors had disappeared Hugh started staging his photos in a long row.

Having quickly deposited most of the dust even further into the plumbing equipment Pete and I were ready for a conducted tour. These, we recognised, were Hugh's babies and we could see his great love of shades and textures in his still lifes, landscapes and even his nudes.

Time went so quickly and that day we had an extra lecture down at the College theatre. But before we could destroy the evidence our tutor returned to lock up. The extraordinary point was that he joined us briefly and, without anyone saying a word, we had to run fast so as not to miss even part of a lecture.

After studies Pete was my great mentor into the realm of classical music. Apart from his playing on the billet piano, not quite to concert pitch, late into most nights, he took me on extended pub crawls around Nottingham: often finishing in the dim catacombs of 'The Trip to Jerusalem.'

Most of those that we stopped in for our half pint had a piano. Pete would quietly slip into the seat and do a few bars of jazz. Then without warning he would change to Chopin, Rachmaninoff or Beethoven. After a pint of beer his playing would express great gusto.

It was while we were in Nottingham that the National Symphony orchestra with piano soloists came to perform for a week. Pete and I were able to attend most nights. After the first evening, Pete and I went to a pub nearby where he was grabbed by members of the Orchestra to perform at some of their rehearsals.

City life - with an excellent billet, a good students' canteen, cinemas, concerts and female company when we had time - was very good. But we had to do extra study into the night. I was even approached after midnight one night to get out some drawing for the student wall magazine the next morning - after all this was War, and REME forbade us to refuse any job!

The final exam came and during the last two days Pete and I were called out for sentence ... but not poor Hugh. Was it his Art Exhibition?

As a final gesture we managed to strike a blow at pomposity. At our final parade for train tickets we so infuriated the SM that he called a hasty extra parade in the Park to give us some marching drill.

He had got us into three ranks and a slightly wobbly line. He was dressed in all his best gear. "By the right!" he yelled, "Quick - MARCH!"

But Anglo/American co-operation had at that moment never been more important for a faint buzz turned into a deafening roar as a squadron of Flying Fortresses flew over. By the time they had gone we had all marched on out of the Park into adjoining woodland - as Pete remarked, "To look for Maid Marian!" It was time to say goodbye.

CHAPTER EIGHTEEN

GOPSALL HALL

I had two glorious days back at home. The meadows were full of spring flowers and butterflies, almost ready for hay cutting, the cattle and pigs on pastures green and lush. Birdsong greeted the smiling dawn.

I walked in human solitude with Pogey, now an elderly ferret, in my pocket, Spring, my lurcher dog, at heel and my old shotgun. I was expected to bring back a couple of rabbits, gutted in the field for my companions, and for my mother to later cook so deliciously with parsley sauce.

Somerset was so peaceful and beautiful in the gentle summer sun. From the top of the farm down the Axe valley the distant cliffs at Seaton Gap revealed the sparkle of the sea: a reminder of my other home - in Orkney, at the other end of Britain. There was a War on!

By studying the rail timetables I managed to work the 'missed connection gambit', and so I landed on Nuneaton station with full kit an hour late. Soon there were four of us. One corporal rang Gopsall and was told to stay put and a lorry would collect us 'as soon as possible'. So we left all our kit on the platform with a large notice 'FIND US AT THE LOCAL'.

The lorry turned up near closing time and the driver found a very happy band of students ensconced in arm chairs who found considerable difficulty in loading their kit into the back of his lorry. The Military Police (Blue Cap) guards at Gopsall Hall patiently observed our fumbling efforts to find our documents. We were then given a good hot meal before being escorted to our beds in some spaced Nissan huts. I found that Pete was in the next bed to mine.

Ancient and Modern!

He said we were in a crazy place - a very good start.

It was surprising that the authorities were so amiable to us, for Pete related how the main intake of the new weekly class of twenty had been met inside the main gate by a 'Padre' and a 'Sergeant Major' who ordered them to dismount, then marched them into the depth of the woods. Here, to their bewilderment, they were issued with hymn books 'Ancient and Modern' from the Chapel and had just formed into a circle when the real Sergeant Major rescued them. Pete reckoned the other one, and the Padre, were Gopsall 'wood sprites'.

No 3 Radio Maintenance School REME Gopsall Hall, revolved around an impressive Georgian mansion - the one-time seat of Lord Waring - two miles from 'nowhere' in gentle countryside. The Staff, offices, and some classrooms were in the main building but the students slept in Nissen huts scattered under the branches of great Cedar of Lebanon trees in the wooded grounds. At the end of May the wood was full of birds and in the hot sun of day they would be busily feeding in the high trees. Copper beeches skirted the wood with the mottled light filtering down camouflaging the huts. Little flower beds sided many huts. The entire School covered about ten acres of buildings, vehicle parks and playing fields, surrounded by a heavily guarded wire fence.

The next morning we all attended the school rollcall with the senior student of each class shouting out 'all correct', apparently without any reference to who was there. Many students had their towels around their necks. The twenty new intake were then required urgently in a bare classroom where we had to first sign a 'Part 11 of the Official Secrets ACT'. Then we had to complete a short written test to see if we had brought our brains with us.

Students could be allocated to various studies. There were the new Canadian 10cm advanced Radars, LW, said to be a mobile Tank radar, IFF Aircraft code identification equipment, Electronic predictors as well as a range of wireless sets, telephone and sound equipment. All students would have to reassemble generators.

Pete and I found ourselves doing all the electrical equipment on Radar Mark 1, Mark 1* and Mark 11 Heavy AA Sites. We were obviously wanted back in Orkney. Both of us had caught the Orkneyitis bug.

The School was a curious mixture of militarism and scholarship. Rumours said the Commandant Colonel was a learned professor who because he wore a

116

beard could not appear before the troops; alternatively that he had no beard but refused to wear a uniform. It might just have been that he hated saluting!

The method of teaching somewhat resembled the early days of North Berwick. We operated in small classes of ten. Here we did hectic forty-five-minute sessions on Radar and IFF theory and circuit studies, mostly in Nissen Huts with windows blacked out and the door locked. It was obvious from the first that our Staff Sergeant instructors had been hand-picked for their witty enthusiasm. We were all swept along rather like swimming in a warm fast-moving tide. The fault finding was turning into a sort of game.

There were also Radars outside and we even did (non-secret) wireless studies sitting on the grass out in the warm sun. In a small shed we gradually dismantled a Diesel Generator which had to be re-assembled and started up on the last day. Learning had never been so easy and satisfying. The one great rule for happiness was always to be on time for each session. I found it impossible not to pay attention. Gopsall would do the rest.

The food was excellent and the ATS domestic and clerical staff provided a ready-made supply of partners for the frequent dances. There were no girl students although I gathered there were a few on Sites in the South of England.

We worked on a nine-to-five basis with free weekends and could not - due to security - have our books for private study. We could go out in our spare time within a five-mile radius.

Many of the staff and students were in the arts and entertainment industry and there were regular cinema, stage shows and school concerts. There was a good library and classes in ballroom dancing. There was a good piano and an organ in the Chapel - another place where Handel was reputed to have composed part of the 'Messiah'. Also a school band - and any other recreational activity that students wanted to organise.

Despite the playing field, grazed by a small flock of sheep, the main physical activity appeared to be walking, and pub crawling, in the surrounding countryside or tearing around the field with very little on in the way of clothes. The main sport soon became apparent - Sergeant Major baiting. The Sergeant Major - a dapper ramrod of a man with a staccato voice and a piercing twinkle in his eye told us he had been a Fusilier but only historians amongst us seemed to know what that was. He was personally responsible for the little flower beds in the wood and several members of his staff tended them with loving care.

Very occasionally the sheep would break out from the field and enter the wood, so when the flowers were at their best he mounted a sheep patrol. But he did not obtain the complete goodwill of the students who, in the dead of night would imitate the souls of lost sheep echoing through the trees, so that he and the patrol would turn out to check that all was well.

There was also an extensive Wall Newspaper with student contributions from obviously professional artists and writers. But how Pete and I combined these two latter activities was one of the highlights of our stay in Gopsall.

Our great sadness was that Hugh, the artist, had not joined us so Pete said that we should try our hand at 'Impressionist' painting. We were gladly given materials by the education sergeant and we started painting the woodland scene in our own 'Monmartre' with our own hut as a Moulin Rouge substitute. We had morning cocoa in the 'Lapin Agile' otherwise known as outside the cookhouse door.

The Sergeant Major eyed us with deep suspicion and Pete often spoke to him in a French accent. Pete had by that time departed from the standard length Army haircut and wore his cap down over one ear.

Shortly after this we saw in a local paper that an Exhibition of 20th Century French Art was to be held in Leicester. The Sergeant Major told us it was outside the limit. So, advised by the Education Sergeant, we made written application to the Colonel and received two passes to spend the Saturday free time in Leicester.

For a couple of hours in Leicester's Art Gallery we absorbed the works of Manet, Renoir, Dufy, Modigliani and their contemporaries. We saw collage and modern sculptures, cubism, impressionism and all the various schools in between. We wished Hugh had been with us as some of the works seemed so simplistic that we could have knocked them up ourselves.

Outside, as we left the gallery, were two huge bomb casings dug out in the city. Pete was able to convince a dear old lady standing with us they were in fact Modern Art sculptures - German of course!

There was a general rule not to read the notices about discipline put up on the Notice Board - I did not know there was one until it was too late.

After Pete and I went to the Art Exhibition we thought the other members of our hut ought to know something about the glories of Modern Art. So on the Monday morning after breakfast we sent someone out to answer all present at rollcall. Pete said if the beds in the hut were turned sideways he and I could mark out some notable reproductions with some coloured chalks on the floor space.

We did one of Dufy's 'harvesting' with blue horses on a yellow background. A lady with one eye - from an early Picasso - and a 'Fish in Stream'. Suddenly the door burst open and our dear Sergeant Major and one of his Staff demanded to know why our hut was not ready for the inspection 'that he had announced at rollcall.' He was in a state of almost speechless fury.

118

Pete did not help matters by pointing out that the SM was standing on his Dufy.

It was then near class time and nothing was allowed to make students absent or late for study. That could lead to instant expulsion from Gopsall. He caught up with us again as we went into lunch and Pete and I received the maximum punishment he could impose: Fire Watching in the Mansion over all of the next weekend. After lunch the Education Sergeant sought our presence and he persuaded Pete to do the writing and I to do the art work for the subsequent Wall Newspaper.

"Sgt Major... you're standing on my DUFY"

So it duly came to pass that we paraded in battle dress, boots and tin hats after lunch on the Saturday under the direction of an Orderly Sergeant, there to take over the red armbands marked 'FIRE' from two members of regular staff. We were handed a card explaining our duties: we were expected to patrol the entire passageways of the Hall and one of us had, once during every twelve hour period, to enter the ATS dormitory area and going through a trapdoor to look around the extensive roof. One of us had to awaken the duty cook on the Sunday. We also had to lookout for fires.

The duty cook was, upon enquiry, the very powerfully built ATS girl whom we had noticed lingering inside the servery at mealtimes. She usually held a

Cook

meat cleaver in her hand and appeared to prop up the door posts. I drew the short straw and had to enter the ATS quarters at 06.00hrs and ensure she was fully awake - otherwise no one would get breakfast and that would be a crime. The Army issued no procedures on 'How to wake duty cooks by numbers'. I adopted the same method I used back on the farm for arousing heifers. This was probably the most dangerous thing I did during the whole war, my only protection being a tin hat and a FIRE armband.

Working for the Wall Newspaper that weekend gave Pete a great opportunity to do a history of Gopsall. I used some painting of the woodland, a pen drawing of the main facade and a set of surrealistic studies of Gopsall in spring, summer, autumn and winter.

But my great inspiration was to do a coloured cartoon of the Sergeant Major attacking the slumbering Camp in the grey light of dawn, accompanied by bats, owls, foxes and other beasties of the night. Because I could not do this work in the main hall I used my unique right to enter the roof where I set up a studio on this glorious summer's day.

The Colonel - so we were told - said we did one of the best papers he had seen. This not only further infuriated the SM but someone on the teaching staff had registered an official complaint that by demanding a tightening-up of general discipline he was interfering with our studies. The following morning when he had quite a goodly number on his rollcall parade he was seen to throw his hat on the ground and jump on it saying that everyone was against him. Pete and I nearly burst into tears.

Our whole stay at Gopsall was a gloriously happy experience in the middle of a ghastly War. Made all the more pleasant as we all got an increase in trade grading and pay.

But our dear SM was, I fear, not out of the woods yet. When the last day came he always held a special important parade at 09.30hrs for the departing brethren to get their train tickets and passes to proceed back to their Units. There was a large notice on the board that no one was to be late for this parade. It was under another large type notice forbidding disfigurement to the trees.

We all packed our kit ready for the lorry but then a senior student among us requested we follow him. 'Once again Dear Friends!' was his remark as we quickly filed into the depths of the wood. Here we observed a long piece of cord dangling down from high up in a Cypress tree. We formed a circle with bowed heads, for traditional rumour told us what was coming.

Last Rites

There was a scream of anger as the Sergeant Major for the second time had lost the class. As he approached, the cord was pulled and a lovely pair of frilly lady's knickers glided down like a great white butterfly to land at his feet. All eyes looked again up the tree. There was a plaque:-

TO THE HAPPY MEMORY OF CLASS GL28.
THEY PASSED THIS WAY in 1943.
RIP.

As the lorry moved out of the School we waved good-bye and he was heard to remark that we were the greatest shower he ever had the misfortune to deal with. That was high praise indeed.

Ain't it dreme in the reme

CHAPTER NINETEEN
TOGO'S ARMY: HOY

In warm late summer weather the journey back to Caldale was very pleasant, even the crossing was moderately calm and we could see little Spanish fishing boats bobbing among the waves. They were said to trade onions for fish caught around the Faroe Islands.

Pete and I were experienced Army travellers. Both of us knew Edinburgh well and we took the opportunity of giving in-depth study to the route. We consulted the RTO clerks more to discover how we could just miss connections rather than just make them, then how to avoid the military train.

It was possible, we learned, to take a civilian day-stopping train up the East Coast of Scotland and catch a boat from Wick to Lyness on Hoy. Southwards the REME would allow us to pay the small difference and take a plane from Kirkwall to Dyce Airport, Inverness, and thus gain a whole day of leave. We explored the cliff way out of the transit camp at Thurso.

It seemed to us that as about half the Radar mechanics were away on leave or courses at any one time it was difficult for the Radio Shop Office to know what was going on. I never even appeared on a payroll.

They just managed to maintain at least one mechanic on each site and the spare men operated from the Caldale Workshop. They preferred volunteers for each position. The Army loved volunteers - some always stayed in workshops. Two were native Orcadians.

So as soon as we shed our boots the next morning outside the Shop, Pete became seated at a bench to do circuit rewiring and soldering. I was out to accompany a colleague and spend the day on Hoy Island. We caught the mail boat from Scapa Pier so as to enjoy a rather magical tour of the battleships and cruisers at their anchorages, before putting into Lyness and being taken to H2 4.5 HAA Site on the heaths behind the Base.

We were not allowed to work on the Set for more than one hour at a time as it was not to be reported out of action. Our job entailed fitting larger bolts and screws to the automatic timed voltage switching in the Transmitter.

I managed to escape out on to the heath and see the full glories of the Alpine/Arctic flora. I found butterwort, grass of Parnassus, Cotton grass and reindeer moss. There were birds everywhere with great skuas, terns, gulls, redshanks, oyster-catchers and even a sighting of the marsh harrier. The pearly light of the Islands stretched out over the Flow and the great Ward Hill behind was even more magical to me after a long spell away.

The resident mechanic saw that we enjoyed the benefits of NAAFI tea breaks and good meals, reserved for special-duty men. We caught a drifter back to Kirkwall and got back to workshops after main work had ceased.

On reaching my hut I found that Pete had gone: he had, I discovered, been lent to the Navy to repair some electric radio-controlled motor boats. I wondered what tricks he would get up to; I was to learn months later. The next morning I put in an application to be sent as a mechanic to Hoy Island.

The next day I actually met a Radio Officer. He was a very quiet rather studious young man, probably straight from University and a short Radar Theory Course. He was seeking to position a new radar-controlled searchlight Site in the area of Lake Stennes.

We were checking for magnetic interference. I did the booking and we were able to find time to look at the fauna and flora, in particular the short-eared owls that nested in that area.

On my return to workshops there was good news. I was to go to H1 as resident mechanic. H1 was the main HAA Site overlooking the Lyness Naval Base and was a very large Site with extra men and a concrete block-making facility. It was rumoured that it was a very strange place; the same Battery had been stationed there for over a year. It had its own mechanic's hut and was known - for some obscure reason - as Togo's Army.

The driver who took me, plus all my kit, which included my personal locked toolbox, from Lyness Pier, told me that this Camp had a welfare man called Goldilocks who would show me to my hut.

Indeed, just after we were waved inside, past the main gate, we picked up Goldilocks, a well-named smiling gunner carrying a piece of paper. He insisted on shaking hands with me and directing the driver to a small hut near the waving aerials of the Radar.

"Welcome to Togo's Army. We hope you will be very happy!" He was I thought carrying informality a bit far.

On the door of the hut was painted the Red Flying Arse'ole, KEEP OUT, and the reproduction from an advertisement 'Is your journey really necessary?' written in Chinese. The key was in the door and inside was an array of metering equipment on a bench beside the stove, a couple of chairs and two beds, one ready for sleeping. I would have to draw some blankets.

Goldilocks explained that my colleague - known as Corp for he had two stripes - had just gone over to the NAAFI to put the wireless set out of action.

"Out of action?" Things were getting strange already.

"Oh yes! The bloody Sergeants claim it for their mess and will collect it shortly."

"So it won't work?"

"You've got it in one" said Goldilocks "They have to send it back to the NAAFI where Corp, or you, will repair it."

"And the NAAFI gets it back again?"

Goldilocks - well named for he seemed never to have met the Regimental barber - hurried away saying something about a raffia class.

Corp duly returned having, he explained, just changed over a couple of similar valves, now quite an established radio trick.

We collected our midday dinner from the cookhouse and ate it at leisure in our hut. After Corp explained that he was due for leave any day, we donned overalls and I carrying my tool-box with me, and Corp with a bit of flex around his neck we toured the Camp.

There were the usual white painted stones marking the track-ways. There was the sunken Command Post with the mechanical predictor - a job for Instruments if it went wrong. There was the highest point with a bored-looking figure standing by the double Lewis Gun.

Centre stage were the four 4.5 in Heavies pointing skywards in their concrete turrets - there was a resident RA Gunfitter to kept the weapons in trim.

We approached these warily as, without outside warning, they had been known to go off. The crack caused a ringing in the ears as one jumped a foot in the air.

Then there were extra huts for making the concrete blocks. Tucked away was the Officers' Mess - to be avoided - where about three officers would usually hide and often drink heavily. There could be a Radio Officer but Corp said he believed he was on the next Site and was useful for bringing the weekly pay, cigarettes and coupons. Corp had been told never to worry the Officer before 11 a.m. as he was late riser. Of course they changed around like the mechanics but most were young, were biologists, and very shy. They could be persuaded to act as a stand-in so that a lone mechanic could have time off. Corp likened them to the rare storm petrels that nested on Hoy.

Finally we had a look at the Transmitter - GL Mark 2 - with its Receiver in the middle of the 'mat'. Chugging away in its own hut was the 60 HP Diesel Generator and the battery charger with the array of fizzing batteries for operating the gun loading mechanisms and as standbys for lighting and Command Post equipment.

We met many of the radar operators and their sergeant, a genial Yorkshireman, who was typical of a man in charge of a squad half of whom would at any one time be fast asleep. The Radar was still out of bounds to those not engaged in its operation - and that included, so I was assured, the Artillery Officers. The Camp could be entered or exited from under the mat which spanned the perimeter, very useful as I was very rarely properly dressed in Army terms.

Corp was also deeply interested in farming and biology as he had worked in the Agricultural Ministry in civilian life and they made up his pay. After dark that evening we were settled in the Radio hut when we could hear some shouting and men running outside our door.

Then Goldilocks put his head around the door. "World challenge ... Bandilock Goat ... boxing ... in the dining hall NOW."

"Better go," said Corp. "They'll want us to fix the spotlight."

We locked the hut and made our way across the darkened Camp, although the aurora was already showing green in the northern sky.

The door to the dining hall was opening and closing, sending shafts of light on to the ground outside as shadowy figures slunk around. I followed Corp inside and under a spotlight were the ropes of a boxing ring. Tables had been rearranged with benches on top to form an arena, the faces of the assembled men shining out like boy scouts at a camp fire. The place smelt of cigarettes and beer. I could see that some men were draped in blankets.

Goldilocks met us at the door and ushered us to two seats - away from the corners as 'we might get wet'. In front of us sat a man with an empty fire bucket and a large poker. I guessed he was the time keeper.

Among those climbing into the ring was a thick set little man with beetle brows and curly black hair. He peered for a few moments into the expectant audience in all directions and waved to the man with the firebucket. The latter then attacked the bucket with his poker bringing the audience to silence.

126

"That's Hackett - the boss" whispered Corp. He was ready to make a speech.

"Ah! Lidies an' gentle - MEN," he bellowed. "Aa t'night we 'ave th' spectacle" (he gazed around into the audience) "of the best boxer in this part of the whole woorld!" He halted to let the fact sink in. "Defend his title in three rounds against another great loc'l hexponent of the fisticuffs. Lidies an' gentle - MEN! In the red corner we 'ave - none other than Gunner Meldrum -

Time!

otherwise known as the BANDI - LOCK GOAT." A pale white skinny little man rose from his corner-seat in the ring and raised his gloves on high for all to see. There was clapping, cheers and shouts of 'Fuck 'em Jock' until another bang on the bucket again brought silence.

"An' in the blue corner, Lidies gentle- MEN we 'ave, Gunner Broom. Otherwise known as the BEAR of Bannock." An enormous man in a black overcoat rose up. Then I realised he was not wearing an overcoat after all but just shorts. He reminded me of a black bear just coming out of hibernation. He swept his seconds aside as he held his great tree-trunk arms straight out to reveal his boxing gloves.

There was loud clapping, laughter and ribald shouts of "Get yer fucking greatcoat off man!"

"Your referee for tonight," continued Hackett, "Gunner Gorrel: known to you bastards as FIXER. Seconds out ... Round ONE." There was another clang on the bucket.

At this FIXER tried vainly to get them to touch gloves but the GOAT was determined to keep his gloves up in defence. Leaning forward he only reached to the hairy middle of the BEAR who appeared to be doing an imitation of a pollarded tree trunk.

While BEAR pivoted at the centre of the ring with his great arms spread like the aerials of the Radar, the GOAT circled him, shadow boxing.

The audience screamed encouragement and advice, not all of which appeared relevant. 'Kick 'im in the bollocks!' ... 'Shoot the bastard!' ... 'Left 'ook to the groin! ....'Watch out for the fucking fleas!' and just ''it 'im!' After a time it appeared to me that the Bear was getting frustrated, it was rather like him swotting a mosquito. He cornered the Goat and drew back his right arm in a wide circular motion; like an angry bull he was intending to sweep the Goat into the air and right out of the ring.

But as the Goat's early extinction looked certain the crashing of the poker on the fire bucket terminated the round. The seconds leapt into the ring and gripping the Bear's arms dragged him back to his corner. Both contestants then had a half bucket of cold water thrown into their faces: probably, I thought, to anger then rather than cool then down.

The second round was announced and was even shorter than the first. The Bear had got the measure of his smaller opponent and the screams of encouragement almost drowned the 'bell'. The seconds had only just time to refill their buckets.

The final round started before the seconds could properly mop up the contestants so that the Goat was seen to body punch the referee at least twice. The Bear swung around, missing his target, so that he collapsed on all fours with the referee even starting the count.

The door opened to silhouette the entry of the Orderly Sergeant just as Gunner Hackett was doing his 'Lidies and gentle - MEN' bit to announce a draw and a re-fight at a later date.

Corp told me that this was in fact the fourth re-fight and that one of the Sergeants had been a bit worried that one of the contestants might, in frustration, try to settle the issue with the Twin Lewis.

So the next day we learnt that Gunner Hackett had 'kindly offered' to announce at all meals that Gunner Meldrum was not to be referred to as the Bandilock Goat in future. He was not asked to say anything else. However he added that nobody should shout 'Bandilock Goat' as Gunner Meldrum had just collected his main course, pudding and cup of char at the cookhouse hatch. Otherwise he would hurl the entire meal, plates and all straight up through the dining hall. An exception was made to apple pie as Gunner Meldrum was particularly fond of apple pie.

The following day I went to have dinner whilst Corp was off to check out a

All except apple pie!

telephone. I sat at the back of the hall. Gunner Meldrum came in with his 'friend' Hackett and had just drawn their food from the hatch when a subdued cry of 'Bandilock Goat' came from somewhere in the hall.

The first plate sailed up the hall like a thrown discus, spraying roast and two veg as it went. Following quickly was rice pudding and a whole cup of hot char. I tended to take my food back to the Radio hut after that.

Because there were more men than on a normal AA Gunsite, the Forces Entertainment Service (ENSA) allowed more lavish shows to visit H1. Goldilocks, under the direction of the Welfare Officer, would ask the 'Madio Wrecs' to see to the lighting and amplifier.

The single artists were allocated a bathroom each. But the dancing girls, the most popular entertainment, were allocated a store room next to the kitchen.

A cunningly constructed row of spy holes had been made to give the Chief Bombardier cook and his invited guests a preview of the girls as they changed. This was why the front two benches were only brought in moments before the curtain went up (sideways). The girls were invariably, by tradition, entertained by the Sergeants Mess. Their frequent inability to stand up straight - let alone dance - added to their popularity.

Men who had managed to have slept for days would even get up for this entertainment. There was, we all suspected, someone high up in Naval circles who would put on a short practice 'red alert' in the middle of these shows. Our Radar showed it was nothing to do with the Germans.

Corp was suddenly collected to go on leave after a week. I was then normally on my own. Goldilocks would frequently visit me in my hut - he was now a Spotter, a sort of night watchman having been demoted from being the Site Gun Fitter. He told me how this came about.

The recoil on big guns was taken up by a plunger operating in an oil cylinder kept under high pressure by compressed air. The oil was topped up through a valve operated by a large lock nut. A special huge spanner was used to turn the nut.

Goldilocks admitted that he forgot that it was a right-hand thread. So by a tremendous physical effort he managed to damage the nut so that a thin jet of oil rose out of the Gun Pit, where only fired shells should normally go. Precisely as this happened he saw an inspecting Officer and his retinue entering the gun pit.

Being a man of great resource he jumped up on to the recoil and stood on the nut. He soon realised that the oil was not going upwards but outwards as a fine spray, hitting the inspection party amidships and giving an oily tidemark right around the pit with its polished rows of stacked ammunition.

129

REME were called to get the gun in action again.

A condition of his Court of Enquiry was that he failed his Trade Test. He was praised for the welfare work he did with the Battery and so was not posted. Goldilocks had unfortunately reasoned that because Radio Mechanics had a set of watch makers tools in our kit we knew something about watch repairs.

Corp taught me two methods before he left. One was to give the watch a good shaking, the other was to remove the back and soak the watch in the hot benzene we used for freeing fine switches in the Radar. It often worked. Really worn-out watches could, I suggested, be incorporated in the concrete blocks.

Goldilocks' flair as a talent spotter manifested itself in his solo performers. He would come to my hut, usually during the evening, when he would give me the low-down on the Togo's Army latest. If it was after midnight we would go and get a tot of rum.

He called me Pa, not because I was a father figure but it just happened to be my initials. "You must see this fellow Pa" he would say as he led me into the backwoods of the camp to some little known hut. Amongst the shows arranged for usually about a five-man audience was the memory man.

One night we went to the corner of a hut where we all sat crossed-legged on blankets. In the centre was a very thin young man who appeared to be in some sort of trance. In front of him was not a Buddha but

Memory man

a high pile of separate sheets of paper. On each sheet was written the detailed weather in London for a day. Goldilocks explained that he had learnt every particular on every sheet.

We each could name a day and time during the last twenty years. The man would then give us the details which we could check from the sheet. After about ten totally correct details - temperature, precipitation, wind direction and speed as well as outlook - he got a one degree error in temperature. We crept away in silence. Goldilocks explained that he would have to go through all the lot again - he had already spent four years to get that far.

Another night I was privileged to attend a song recital. Four of us sat on the edges of the beds around the central stove in an obscure Nissen hut as the high wind whistled outside. On an upturned box sat the performer - wielding the poker. There was silence apart from an occasional snoring for it appeared everyone else was fast asleep if not in terminal hibernation. Goldilocks just introduced him as Jordy. He began a slow rhythmic gentle beating of the stove pipe:-

They're moving father's grave to build a sewer.
They're moving him regardless of expense!
They're moving his remains
To make way for tenants' drains,
To suit the needs of local residents.'

There was a sort of sobbing note in his voice as his song went on to relate how the old man would 'Dress up in a white sheet and haunt every shithouse seat and only let them shit when he would allow.' The details of how chronic constipation would decimate the population were related with almost a feeling that it was Jordy's own dad.

As the song ended there was subdued applause and as we left Jordy was seen to get back into his bed.

One very dramatic demonstration was by 'Flasher', a well-constructed lad with reputed high sexual drive. I was fetched late at night to a distant hut where Flasher was to be shown a series of photos taken by a new member posted to the Battery who had lived in Sierra Leone. These showed the local natives in active sexual coupling. Apparently their form of busking.

Flasher's fame arose from his reputed ability to lift a sand-filled firebucket with his erect penis. In Orkney the opportunity of sexual thoughts was limited due to our normally 'monastic' life. After several attempts Flasher succeeded but the ensuing round of laughter and applause disturbed him so that half a bucket of sand had to be swept up.

Goldilocks reckoned it was cruel to keep all these men in Camp without the sight of women - except on the weekly film show for those off duty. So a weekly tea dance was arranged using an old gramophone which I coupled to the NAAFI amplifier. About twenty Wrens were indented for from the Lyness Base and these would be dropped off at the door of the NAAFI for two hours when the lorry would return and they would be counted on again.

I stayed to operate the system and play the group of Victor Sylvester records provided. Tea was provided from a tea bucket and mugs sent over from the cookhouse. Entry from the Camp was rationed by ticket only and the proceedings were very respectable - and not very exciting.

Goldilocks had developed a wonderful system to have a day off in Kirkwall about every tenth day. He had persuaded the Welfare Officer to sanction the start of classes to do raffia work. The only place to buy raffia was in a stationer's in Kirkwall and Goldilocks was very careful not to buy more than a week's supply at a time. So he would pick a fine day to set out by lorry and boat with a list of requirements.

There were men in the camp doing handicrafts and modelling for the Annual Exhibition in Kirkwall. There were talks and lectures; I was even persuaded to give a talk on modern farming.

Then someone bet Goldilocks a pound note that he could not get Gunner Meldrum, the Goat, into Admiral Fraser's Annual Red Cross Naval Ball as a guest. The planning for the operation was done in the Radio Hut because of the tight security needed. Tickets could only be obtained through the Major's (Togo's) direct line to the Admiral's Office.

The Camp suffered a series of minor 'mishaps' and 'accidents' during the next few days which brought Togo momentarily out of his office ... while a man with golden curls concealed under his cap was doing the dusting. Two men - the Goat and the Fixer - had to get replacement new uniforms for those damaged by the concrete-block machine.

With two tickets and new uniforms both men had to be scrubbed and their boots polished. They were inspected by Goldilocks and were smuggled out of the Camp under the Radar mat. Two referees shadowed them down to the Ball.

They did get in but said that after grabbing a free drink they fled for the others were all Officers. Goldilocks got his pound.

All too quickly I realised I would soon have to depart as my next leave was due; always a bit dicey as I was not on anyone's payroll. When I told Goldilocks this he had a great idea - which could get both of us shot if it was found out.

He was a wonderful mimic and could imitate Mr Churchill giving one of his great boosting speeches to the Nation. The Camp was wired up to the central wireless set in the NAAFI. Goldilocks wanted me to rig up a secret concealed microphone into the circuit and write a bogus Churchillian speech about Togo's Army.

I wrote the speech and got a spare microphone. I would only allow him to carry out his plot after I had had time to get

"Never... in the field..."

home. I never heard the speech but I was told that General Montgomery visited H1 while I was on leave. They believed Goldilocks and many others were posted overseas.

CHAPTER TWENTY
THE BALLOON GOES UP

Goldilocks saw me off from H1 and I crossed the Flow to spend the night at Caldale. The next day I caught the civilian De Haviland Rapide plane out of Kirkwall Airport in glorious late autumn sunshine to land at Inverness. We flew above the shoreline to see seals basking and with magnificent views over the Highlands of Scotland. I had also gained a day's leave.

For my return journey I went by civilian train to Wick and then to Caldale via Lyness. For a time I alternated between working at a bench and going out on jobs, mostly as one of a pair. I learnt that the Black Crag Radar had been blown over but the other lone Radars were still operational. Another had been damaged by lightning strike. Although workshop life was more comfortable for it had always to be dry, warm and still for the delicate bench work, I soon got the call of the wild. Then I had some infuriating news.

Pete, late of the Nottingham and Gopsall Bohemians, had been sent to the Navy. They, perhaps wisely, decided to do without him at the last moment, but they never told Caldale. So his whereabouts only came to light months later. He had set up a civilian wireless repair business and was using Army spares. Red sparks would get him food and lodging at any AA Site without question. He also had civilian friends in Kirkwall. It was his punishment that annoyed me.

He had been 'sentenced' to be Site Mechanic at Tommy Tiffy in far Deerness. The Radar was on a cliff overlooking a large kittiwake colony and there were great banks of wild lupins growing there in the spring. A wonderful place to see the wildlife.

The Radar control gearing had been damaged in a winter gale and he had rung up the Workshop and asked that I do the repairs. The lorry took me to the end of a track and I had to finish the journey on foot to the Site.

I found a delighted Pete conducting an art class - a still life. The Radar receiver was lashed down by tough ropes at the end of the aerial framework. A gale was blowing and it was difficult to stand in the open. Beyond sleeping the operators spent their time eating - the rations being supplemented by fish caught further along the coast and eggs from a nearby croft.

I completed the repair but I knew I would have to test it so I got the lads to release the ropes. It worked all right but the Set was rocking so fast in the gale that it took me half an hour to jump out. The Set had to be tied down in high winds as it was not only impossible to get aboard but there was a danger of someone joining the kittiwakes.

On my return to Caldale I realised that I was not seeing enough of the outlying Sites - indeed at H1 I never seemed to have any time entirely to myself. We had a few Radio Officers in the Workshop Mess. I was told that the Captain in charge of the Radio Shop was a university professor of biology. I had briefly seen him once at a distance.

So I wrote a letter to him asking to be banished to a lonely site where I could finish my agricultural correspondence course, write a book and study the fauna and flora. I handed it in to Claude at the office, who had previously suggested that I try shooting the Colonel.

Within an hour I was packing my kit. I was to do balloon calibration as assistant to a corporal known as Sid, who was a sort of legendary figure who had visited most gunsites with his balloon. I would find him at a gunsite at Longhope - known to the Army as 'Losthope' - on the Island of South Walls approached by a causeway at the eastern end of Hoy Island.

I located him on Site H4 where he had taken over from the Site Mechanic who was on leave. He was not in any way artistic, nor particularly knowledgeable about the Island wild life but had, I soon gathered, built up a small egg-and-cheese export business to England. He took his job very seriously as he did not wish to lose it. Pre-war he had been a Bristol insurance salesman. He was an ex-Royal Engineer and had been a Dunkirk harrier and had been digging out bodies in the London Blitz. He had a wife and baby son. He was quite willing to take full responsibility for the job so I could relax with my other interests.

The problem was that calibrating with a Mark VI Kite Balloon could not be undertaken in winds above 15 knots, when there was a likelihood of lightning or when the Radar was on watch. So Sid reckoned we would be lucky - or unlucky, which ever way you looked on it - to work more than two days a month, especially in Orkney where it was quite possible to get both east and west gales on the same day. As a Radio Officer had to monitor the readings, work was about as likely as tossing three sixes with dice.

The Calibration Officer was a learned biologist Captain, known as Doc. He was expected - so Sid said - to see us once each month.

Sid was highly self-disciplined and I found it quite easy to fill our days, with never an idle moment. We would usually get up for the 08.00hrs breakfast, having had a quick look at the Radar. At a possible parade time we would check on the balloon, if it was inflated, and see to any damage to the picket and wire bed. Sid would get a weather forecast from the Command Post. He would then establish that there was no calibrating that day.

Depending on the weather, Sid and I would set out for the Crofts where we would invariably get asked for a cup of tea and a chat. Sid would arrange for eggs and cheeses to be picked up, usually by Army vehicles. Although he had no ready sense of humour Sid always talked as if we were still in the First World War. He promised to see that the Kaiser was captured and I always said I would help him, although I thought it improbable that we would find him on an Orkney croft. The only wood to chop was washed up on the beaches. (The Kaiser was said to have spent his last days chopping wood)

We walked miles along the shore and over cliffs where we would climb down to visit caves and collect coloured driftwood on the shoreline for Sid to use in his hobby of making beautiful marquetry trays. We had to watch out for the Gloops, sunken caves, on the east cliffs. I was soon rapidly finishing my Agricultural correspondence course and always got permission to light a fire in the NAAFI and draw up a chair and table even if it was out of bounds to the rest of the Camp.

There were some five Sites on Hoy, and as the days lengthened in spring I was able to study almost the whole of the Island. We visited Togo's Army and I discovered that Goldilocks had been posted with all the surplus men.

When Sid went on leave, and a course, I found myself at H4 on South Walls. This Site was unique. It had the usual four heavy AA guns and a Mark II Radar but it also had the latest Mark III Canadian Radar - working on 10cms - which consisted of two units. The first, the ZPI (Zone Position Indicator) showed all flying objects on a map of the entire Islands. The other was the APF (Accurate Position Finder) where a cursor could pick up a target and relay it through an electronic predictor direct to the guns.

To keep this lot working, REME had a Staff Sergeant Artificer and four other mechanics. There was an Officer on the next Site and he used to come and sit with us and have a chat, and hand out pay, free cigarettes and coupons, usually about once a week. He was also unique for he claimed to have been a dentist who got on REME Radar by some clerical error.

As the Mark 111 was not fully operational I was to spend most of my time on this equipment, studying the circuit diagrams which were, as usual, chained to the Set. The Staff Sergeant was also a bit of an athlete and he and I used to run the two miles to a rocky swirling pool along the Pentland Firth, dive in and then run back. This was all the more pleasant as swimming in the Pentland Firth was forbidden to all ranks. We assumed most people thought we were civilians.

The REME had most of a Nissen Hut which the mechanics used as a workshop and sleeping place. All the testing equipment was on a bench by the stove and the door had the usual sign KEEP OUT EXCEPT ON BUSINESS. Displayed outside was the REME badge, the Red Flying Ars'ole, the Chinese for 'Is your journey really necessary'. The motto NON ILLGITIMI CARBORUNDUM EST (don't let the bastards grind you down) and two large crossed red, yellow and blue paddles with the motto 'SEMPER IN EXCRETUM'(Always in the shit!).

All this adequately reflected the rather lunatic atmosphere of those inside. Like most mechanics they welcomed the comparatively gentle Army life to recuperate from leave and courses and the travelling entailed.

Behind the concrete-block wall that divided the hut lived the Artillery Bombardier Gunfitter: I would have regarded him at first as a dangerous lunatic. They even called him Banger. His face, hands and his entire body were covered in scars due, my colleagues said, to his hobby - and not the vagaries of War. He claimed to have blown himself up twice and, my colleagues thought, he was working up for a third time - and he was only a few yards away!

He had a passion for collecting explosives. He would take a pinch of cordite from the charges of shells and would take 303 rounds to pieces and store the charge. It was claimed that he had several boxes of explosives next door. All this was much more alarming as his tools included the largest blowlamp I had ever seen .... AND ... he was reputed to work it on petrol.

He obviously suffered from a brand of Orkneyitis and he had a real affinity with other neo-mechanics and used to join us for in-hut meals collected from the cookhouse. Food was as usual more than adequate and the method of

136

Balloons require six men!

cleaning the plates was to put them on the grass outside the door. Almost the entire population of seagulls were in sighting distance; the sky would blacken in a matter of seconds and the plates were 'clean'. However the birds were not respecters of mealtimes.

A type of bird scarer was being developed when I arrived which would, if possible, be designed not to kill the birds - or anyone else. It was found that the birds could not be fooled that easily - and it was using up the explosives.

Then one morning Banger announced that he did not think that Orkney was getting a fair share of the War so he had decided to declare 'War' on the REME. He handed us half of the Thunder Flashes he had collected after the annual 'battle' when the Commandos were allowed to 'attack' the Camps. He said we were allowed to use blowlamps.

This did not prove very successful as he managed to put a Thunder Flash down our stove pipe which meant our having to re-clean some of our delicate metering equipment. We in our turn had put mains voltage on our door handle and 'greatly surprised' our own Officer on an unexpected visit.

It was then decided that both parties should try to develop a rocket. A piece of piping was duly supported at an angle of some forty-five degrees between two wooden posts. It had a welded tail fin and was filled with a special cordite mix. The first firing caused it to do a figure of eight and shower the place with sparks.

By this stage Sid had returned and we had to take the stored balloon kit to the other side of Hoy. We inflated the Balloon from the 6cwt gas cylinder REME obtained from the RAF Balloon Barrage Stores near the Lyness Base.

We had just settled in when Sid was sent to Pomona to start a second calibration unit. I was alone for a time, but the Site mechanic and I shared jobs. We did no calibration.

Now that it was spring we left Hoy and stored our balloon kit to take over the new set of equipment on Pomona. It was a fairly leisurely business as we also acted as Site mechanics for most of the time. I found handling the balloon great fun and, when Sid was in Kirkwall, I often dispensed with the rule that six men should always handle the balloon to and from its bed.

On the farm I often had to lead cattle on a halter and I found a balloon behaves in a similar manner. There were rumours that one mechanic had jumped right over a Nissen hut before he was seen and put back at the bench with a threat that £70 could be stopped from his pay if he lost a balloon.

'Laughing' gulls

As we came to May we arrived back on the St Mary's road again. Orkney was certainly at its most beautiful and interesting.

There was an exercise when the Commandos attacked the camp. Everyone was armed, some with thunder flashes, but apparently they were detected. However Sid said we should take no chances and we stayed in our hut with a cup of tea ready. Sid claimed that no one could resist that ... and I respected his shrewd knowledge of human nature.

Those men returning from leave in the South of England all spoke of the tremendous build up of American and British troops. Something was bound to happen.

CHAPTER TWENTYONE
D-DAY DAWNS

In 1944 the tide of War was strongly in our favour. Allied armies were sweeping the enemy back in every theatre of conflict. Officially it was claimed that since the advent of the Radar the Scapa Flow defences had never been breached. Certainly most men on the AA Camps believed that they would never fire their guns in anger.

With Sid in charge I was able to make frequent visits to my civilian 'family' in Kirkwall. They were an extended Orkney family of three generations called Scollay. They had 'adopted' four roving Radar mechanics and their kindness was unbounded. They were the most delightful people I met during the whole War. They had never been to England.

As the days lengthened the surrounding heathland became a carpet of low-lying spring flowers, chiefly butterwort, grass of parnassius, cottongrass and squill. There were also low heathland grasses, willows and tiny pearlworts. The calls of the curlew, oyster catcher, redshank and the ever present gulls filled the air. Above came the strange 'drumming' of the snipe and the occasional call of duck or geese. The interaction of sky, islands and sea produced a soft pearly light during daytime before the green diaphanous swaying curtains of the northern aurora. Orkney could be very beautiful and peaceful.

Along the Base the barrage balloons could be imagined as keeping the low islands from sinking into the waters. Dotted across the vast waters of the Flow were the larger ships of War, dressed in their confusing camouflage. Little boats scuttled about rather like waterboatmen on a pond - each moving boat produced a wake resembling a silver thread.

The gunsite itself was normally quiet with the Radar slowly revolving as it vainly searched the almost empty sky. All our planes now had an IFF (indicator friend or foe) transponder. Often small planes, probably 'String Bags', would fly low into the little Fleet Air Arm base west of Kirkwall at Grimsetter.

But the Orkney weather was subject to rapid change. The wind would rapidly increase with lashing rain or sleet. It was often difficult to stand without leaning at a ridiculous angle from the ankles. As the eye of the low pressure system passed over there was a lull as the winds backed before producing a gale in the opposite direction. But it was good fresh air and the huts were warm as was the Radar. I found the operators a particularly quiet friendly lot.

Life was certainly not as hard as on the pre-war farm. Army food varied from good to excellent - strangely Caldale was among the best - and I had been known to eat two full dinners at a sitting.

We had no military training or drill. They relied on us to keep fit - if we wanted. The way to get out of uniform was to put on running kit - as long as we had identity discs around the wrist and neck - and run anywhere the fancy took us. I was told not to go swimming or cliff climbing alone but could often find a companion in the same position.

Hello!

Life on these Sites seemed to be particularly delightful in the spring of 1944. A couple of the operators had volunteered to go down to the South of England to train as invasion troops but had been sent back as physically unfit. Their tales of the training were horrific. I knew my old West Somerset Artillery Battery now bore the 'all seeing eye' of the Guards Armoured Division.

In mid-May there was a midget submarine scare in the Flow and most spare men patrolled with rifles. Sid and I walked along the shore below the Camp to see if we could see some dogfish or perhaps a common seal.

Then all courses, leave and letters out were stopped. We knew that D-Day was nigh.

In June we could sense expectancy in the air with the great Warships sending out plumes of smoke. Battle groups would creep out in the night and by the

4th June we seemed to be guarding very little. We read the papers and listened to the wireless. D-Day - the greatest seaborne invasion of all time - was on June 6th. Although storms struck the English Channel that day Orkney was at its most peaceful.

M3 carried on as usual. We seemed very short of Radio mechanics and the Radio Officer would don overalls and stand in for me on a half day off a week if Sid was away. Unfortunately he decided to examine the base-gearing one day; I was told that seeing some feet protruding an operator had grabbed them, and assuming it was me exclaimed, 'Come out, you silly bugger, that's not the place to sleep'. Officers should not dress up as other ranks. Finally Sid went off and left me with the balloon.

For three more months I moved very slowly from site to site. Life went on as usual. Courses and leave were resumed. All went well until I phoned Workshops to know when I could go on leave. They referred me to the Pay Office who told me I had left the Islands some time previously. When I disputed it and said I had been on calibration they told me Doc was away on a course and they would check my story on his return.

I had achieved the distinction of being totally disowned by the REME. A week later Doc turned up with my replacement. I was to have a fortnight's leave immediately and, as I should not have been on calibration for so long, I would return to No. 3 Radio School at North Berwick - for a month's Refresher Course - before being re-issued to the Caldale Workshops. Thus I would not return to Orkney until after Christmas 1944.

CHAPTER TWENTYTWO
SOLO ACT

I found that the School at North Berwick had lost some of its magic. Some of the equipment had even come off the secret list. As I had in fact never been away from Site repairs I found the course very easy, although there were a few modifications to the equipment that had not reached Orkney. There was a feeling of guilt amongst some of the students that while the Allied armies were battling furiously on all fronts we were sitting at desks studying circuits and working office hours.

Two had even applied to be Officers and had spent two days at a WOSB (War Office Selection Board) learning military etiquette. When they discovered that the only commissions available were in the anti-tank Regiments or the Pioneer Corps their zeal had mysteriously evaporated. We were not allowed to revert to our old jobs.

I had the pleasure of spending Christmas day at a Radio school. Students were free from all duties. On a gunsite the telephones and the Radar somehow had a great tendency to require repair during any sort of celebration. Probably because all electrical equipment was strictly tee-total and rebelled if wetted with beer or spirits.

By the beginning of 1945 I was again doing a spell in Caldale Workshops. They were short staffed so I had to go out to Site repairs alone. Many of my old colleagues had left. I put in for a job of Site Mechanic.

As luck would have it I found myself back at M3 outside Kirkwall. The old Set was creaking a bit with age and had been heavily screened to protect it from interference from the Battleships Anson and Howe parked opposite in the Flow.

The Radar operated around the clock with a few short breaks for me to do testing. At this stage of the War I got my first reprimand from the Chief at Workshops. During one evening the operators reported smoke coming from the back of the transmitter and the main fuse had blown. I rushed over

Radar repairs!

and found that the anode resistor of the main transmitter valve - working at 60 Kilovolts - had burnt out. I reported the Set out of action and rang Workshops as I had a replacement valve but no spare resistor.

I received a rocket as I had not paused to realise that if I robbed the Set of all the safety 'debollocking' resistors these could be used (at a risk to myself) to just keep the Set in action.

Another interesting fault was when I was called out to tune up the amplifier in the Receiver. Strangely it worked correctly while I was inside the back of the working Set but as soon as I came out the fault recurred. I rang the Shop who said they could get me a replacement panel in four hours' time. So I got a book and wiring myself into the Set, sat reading - and countering the quips of the operators - until a colleague arrived with the replacement panel from Workshops.

We followed the progress of the War on the wireless or from those returning from leave. We heard about Hitler's V1 Doodlebugs and the V2 rockets. The RAF balloon barrage had left the Islands as had the searchlights. Moving heavy guns would be more difficult we reckoned.

Then suddenly at 22.00hrs in the evening, when all except the duty operators, the guards on the gate and a roving spotter were in bed, we had a very noisy caller. Banging on the hut with a stick and swinging the door open, he proclaimed that operations were ceasing immediately; the Battery was stood-down and would be leaving at dawn. Reveille would be at 05.00hrs. Everyone was woken up: an almost unheard of event in Orkney.

No-one slept again that night for most of the men had a lot of packing to do. It was still dark when they had their last breakfast. I knew this movement did not apply to me so I just dressed - I always wore pyjamas at night - and lay on my bed just inside the door.

At 06.00hrs lorries rumbled into the camp and the operators were called for.

I stood by the door and shook hands solemnly with each of them as they filed out. I felt sad as I had been a gunner once and knew of their camaraderie.

As soon as they had all gone I walked around the deserted Site to the plaintive call of a single seagull. They had left everything. The guns still pointed skywards with the shells neatly packed in layers in the gun pits. The Lewis gun was still in place. The command post with the Predictor was empty. The generator was silent and the Radar moved idly in the breeze. It was a glorious spring day, and I could see a large troopship moving across the Flow from Scapa Pier with the wash like a silken cord trailing behind.

Poor Puss!

I lay on my bed listening to my wireless when, an hour later, a cat hurtled by and a shot rang out just outside the part-opened door. A young Officer peered in wielding a revolver, obviously startled to see a man who had perhaps ignored orders. I spared him any confusion: "REME Radio !" I exclaimed without moving. He just closed the door and resumed his deadly mission of shooting the Camp cats. The battle lasted about half an hour and I saw he had two assistants to inter the bodies.

When he left another 15cwt lorry arrived and dropped two lads off at the cookhouse. I was relieved to find that one was a cook and they told me they would take a few days to clear out the foodstuffs, and we could do our best to lessen the task by eating as much as possible.

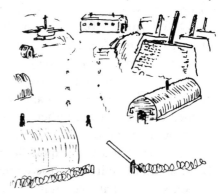

I had no REME instructions; they could have 'lost' me again. Having drawn a blank at the Officers' Mess to find a Radio Officer I rang workshops and they told me to stay with the Set.

I remained near the Radar and paid it visits as I had the keys. I went over to the cookhouse around meal times and they provided substantial meals.

I kept within sigh of the perimeter of the Camp and on the third day I had a visit from one of our experts, Armament Sgt. Major Fisher, whom I once met as an instructor. He had a marvellous idea, worthy of the best traditions of REME radio.

He had been appointed acting Radio Officer for the four nearby Sites. He had taken quarters in the Artillery Radar Operators' school in a sheltered bay near St Mary's. He had arranged for our four Sets with their mechanics to join him. A skeleton staff of two general duty men and two ATS cooks would remain at the School.

So for the next week we put the wheels back on the eight Radar units and a large REME recovery Scammel Lorry winched them to the road and took them to the sandy beach below the School.

The idea, so our Sgt Major told us, was to recondition the units and treat them with anti-fungus compound for service in the Far East. But we never saw the spare parts or the anti-fungal solution. So we used to parade, usually in swimming trunks, at about 10.00hrs each weekday and swim in the shallow warm bay with a family of common seals, or get a lift into Kirkwall, about six miles distant.

Going on leave or courses was used by REME to redistribute its personnel. Every time I left the Islands it meant I lost my job and I had to spend some time at Workshops before getting fixed up again. So the time came for our SM Fisher to take his turn for leave. Questions must inevitably have been asked.

The School was closed down and we, and our beloved old Radar Sets, were trundled back to grace the yard outside the Caldale Workshop.

REME was responsible for dismantling all the Sites and Anti Aircraft guns littering the area outside the gunshop. Vehicles gathered outside their respective shops and predictors and range finders lingered, occupying any odd space. The Workshops had been sited amongst the great concrete blocks of the WW1 Airship Base and the buildings sprawled with the apparent aim of lessening the effect of bombing. Mud was a factor of life at the Camp of (someone suggested) a thousand men at its peak. There wasn't much room to work in the Radio Shop. So the policy was to get a job card to do some - real or imaginary - work on a Set and then, as long as one kept out of sight, no-one seemed to worry. It was rather like working in a grave-yard.

I know some of us read books, listened to the wireless, did a correspondence course or even did wood modelling. With breaks for meals and visits to the NAAFI and the shit-house the working day went quickly. There were no night call-outs or work at weekends.

As it appeared that we might not be in Orkney for much longer, I spent many long evenings with the 'family' in Kirkwall. My favourite member was the aged grandmother who came down from the most northern Island of Papa Westray. We swapped tales of farming and crofting and she would tell me about the old times of whaling and fishing. I would also meet the two 'adopted sons' left on the Island at that time.

We also went to cinema shows. There was a café with a tennis court and I sometimes played after midnight. There was a sixteen-year-old daughter whom they trusted out at night in the company of Roger, a colleague. He would always solemnly ask her father's permission with the words, "I can assure you Sir, that my intentions are entirely dishonourable."

The father would invariably smile and reply "I am sure they are young man, I would trust you with her anywhere." I don't think he or the girl really noted what he said!

The REME did not like us coming past the gate guard after 22.30hrs but we often went via the 'scenic' route or came in after midnight when the guard would be either asleep, playing cards or inside the guard hut. I knew there was an elaborate warning system for the approach of stray Generals, Orderly Officers or sundry unknown 'enemy' vehicles.

Thus came the rather protracted end of the War in Europe for us. All the sweat, blood and tears had passed us by. Nothing much happened at the Camp but a notice said we would all get a couple of extra days leave. The 8th of May was called V.E. Day. As a colleague remarked to me as I walked out to spend the day in Kirkwall, "I really don't know what all the fuss is about ...you'd think there had been a bloody war on."

CHAPTER TWENTYTHREE
TIDYING UP

A feature of the REME was that we rarely saw an Officer at Workshops. I did not know who they were except from rumour. The AA Workshop Company also had a number but most of us had to look up documents to say what it was. But we did strangely have a Regimental Sergeant Major who was very much on view. He was fanatical about guns and could be seen wearing grimy overalls, usually creeping around the innards of a big gun at the Gun Shop.

Now the European War was over all the equipment from the Gunsites and Radar posts was crowded within the confines of Caldale. In order to break the claustrophobia some Officer, we presumed, hit on the idea of a gentle Workshop route march. Two miles to Finstown and back. He had probably been told that most personnel spent long hours in bed asleep and only moved a few yards from bed to the cookhouse or bench so a little gentle exercise would do them no harm.

There were some skilled craftsmen who were unfit even by civilian standards. I knew of one who had one eye and another two who were on special diets. Several more were exempt from all parades of any sort.

However, the rest - including many old men over thirty - were ordered to go on a special morning roll-call. There was the usual confusion, for when names were called there were shouts of 'Leave!', 'Course!', 'Posted last year!', or even 'The bugger's dead!' I was there mainly for the entertainment value, as a check would have revealed I was not on their payroll.

No one quite knew what pace we were to adopt. Many had not marched for years and some, I suspected, had never marched at all. We wore overalls and finally several hundred men got into roughly three ranks. The authorities were a little dubious of the outcome, for two large flatbed lorries were to follow the column - to 'pick up the dead!' according to the drivers.

The RSM was seen wearing his uniform and gave the order 'Quick March!' He did not seem very enthusiastic and was heard to mumble something to himself.

I had kept very fit for I did long walks in the hills of Hoy and regularly walked in and out of Kirkwall. I also did hard farm labour on my leaves.

The actual four-mile route walk took about eighty minutes but it was three hours later before all the 'bodies' were brought in by lorry. It must have been plain, even to the REME hierarchy, that men should be encouraged to get fit before an encore was staged.

Thus was introduced a series of seven Basic Individual Fitness Tests. Every man was issued with a test card with the seven tasks. Dotted in the heathland around Caldale, test centres were set up. As an alternative to pretending to be active in the workshop we could go along to a centre of our choice and try out or take the test. It was typical of REME at its best.

Thus I could try to run a mile in six minutes, run one hundred yards in about twelve seconds, walk a mile in twenty minutes. Or I could chin the bar six times, long jump twelve feet and high jump four feet or do twenty press-ups. Marks were given for bettering the minimum. The entire event was highly amusing and enjoyable to all concerned.

It had not escaped the notice of our superiors that most men, (we were fifty percent N.C.O.s in the Radio shop) sadly lacked the ability or desire to be soldiers in the normally accepted sense of the word. Our Officers appeared to have come straight from civvy street - the Radio Officers from university - so they appeared to be exempt from all these developments.

So REME took over a small abandoned infantry camp on high ground to the North of Caldale and well out of sight of prying eyes. Here they ran a seven-day Regimental Course. Food and refreshments would be sent out from Caldale by lorry.

It quickly got back to Caldale that this course was more entertaining than anything put on by ENSA. The star of this Show was the sergeant drill instructor - known affectionately as Sgt Jock McHaggis. His patter and miming ensured that the dominant noise coming from the camp was laughter ... coupled with some very weird cries and a few minor explosions.

It was on 10th June 1945 that I, and 19 other instrument and Radar mechanics, left Caldale by lorry for the hills. We were duly welcomed by Sergeant Jock who started the course by giving us a little talk on elementary military foot drill as we sat on our kit-strewn beds in our hut.

The students of this class, he had been told, had spent the last five years dodging the column, swinging the lead, hitting the deck, going around the bend or even up the pole. So it may have escaped our notice that drill commands were no longer given in English or even Scotch. They were in the language of 'Milispeak' - derived not from Urdu but from early Bullshit.

So he would use this language throughout the course and demonstrate not only how each position should be attained but, perhaps more importantly, how it should not be done. Lesson No 1 would be how to stand upright, a position assumed on the command 'Sten...shun!!' Sergeant Jock was a wiry small man with an easily contorted body - rather, I thought, like Houdini. His body seemed to lean slightly backwards from over his heels and his bodily

Eel grass!

movements could well be described as staccato as indeed was his vocal delivery. I wondered where the REME had found him or whether the REME processed him themselves from a standard model.

He said he realised that in Orkney, where the wind was rarely less than gale force, the natural stance of a soldier was legs and arms spread with knees bent to lower the centre of gravity, pivoting from the ankles at an alarming angle to prevent the body from being blown over. Rather, he thought, in the manner of our first stone age ancestors at Scarrabrae in the North. In moments of rare comparative calm a line of men at the correct 'Sten...shun!!' position should sway about rather like eel grass on a rocky shore. We all eyed the demonstration with considerable interest.

We then went outside for our first practical: 'The GEFFILIN'.

"Every military manoeuvre starts with the GEFFILIN," said Jock. "You might have met it in the old days as 'Fall in' or 'Get fallen in'."

"Or get in some semblance of order!" I volunteered.

"Aye! That's right" said Jock. "Getting from the mooching around position

151

on the Parade ground to three ranks ... not two or four ... three will do."
There were murmurs of 'three'.

"Now when I shout 'GEFFELIN' I want a cloud of dust and a row of statues."

We practiced this for some minutes with special reference to the mooching. The shout of GEFFELIN being taken up by a solitary oyster catcher above and a black grouse in the nearby heather.

During our first morning we progressed to the subsequent commands of 'RYE...TIP' to get us in some sort of straight lines and the turning commands of 'RYE...TIP', 'LEP...TIP' and 'ABBA...TIP'. Jock ably demonstrated how easy it was to slash a boot on these manoeuvres and how the ABBA...DIP could cause a man to either fall over or pirouette on one heel.

At the end of our first session Jock explained the method of ending all manoeuvres. He would shout 'SQ...AAD' twice to gain our attention. This was usually said in a squeaky voice. Followed by the 'DIZZ...MIZZ', translated this really meant Bugger Off! On this command men would mooch away from the parade ground.

During our first cocoa break Jock explained how the course worked. Each day we spent the morning studying the parts. In the afternoon we would polish the whole manoeuvre to be ready for an Officer's inspection. If the Officer did not turn up by 15.30hrs We would do the DIZZMIZZ and be free for the day as from 16.00hrs.

When someone asked how often he turned up Jock said he had only come along once, "but you never know with these buggers!"

Advanced rifle drill

The following day we did the drills with the standard .303 Lee Enfield Rifle. We again had a new vocabulary to learn. There was the 'SLOP...HAMS' the 'DER...HAMS' and 'SENT...HAMS'. We also practiced the 'STIPI...HICE' and the 'S..TEASY'.

Sergeant Jock demonstrated the hazards of drills while carrying a rifle. How it was possible to 'brain' the man standing next in line, how easy it was to drop the rifle and even to get enmeshed with a loose sling.

We then donned overalls to practice firing positions both standing and prone

152

although we had no ammunition so lives were not in danger. I managed to get special mention as a rifle must never be carried over the arm in the manner of a shot gun. We also learned how to clean a rifle and how to let an Officer examine the inside of the barrel without poking his eye out.

The third day was taken up with revision and a very special treat after dinner. Sergeant Jock produced a box of Practice Piat Anti Tank Mortars. These were to be stuck on the end of a rifle and fired at a tank. But as he was unable to produce a tank and the round carried no explosive charge he produced a few pieces of galvanised sheeting. We all had a chance to fire the weapon from the prone position. The Officer, perhaps wisely, did not turn up that day.

Subsequent days were devoted to handling the Bren Gun ... a pale shade of my old Bren course back in 1940. It was now more like a Chinese puzzle with witty commentary.

We went to a lake where we actually fired a burst each from a Sten Gun. One student reckoned he had shot a sea trout ... but this was not confirmed as we were attacked by midges at the lakeside and beat a hasty retreat.

It was fine but windy weather during the course, and several of us were able to examine the fauna and flora of the area in some detail. In the absence of an Officer, Jock himself held the 'passing out' parade. The final word of the course was the DIZZMIZZ.

When I returned to Caldale the great topic of conversation was the General Election. Voting was by proxy for Servicemen on 5th July with the results to be declared on the 26 July.

Early rifle use 1940

CHAPTER TWENTYFOUR
POLITICS: THE GENERAL ELECTION

When I arrived back at the Workshops at Caldale I found election fever at its height. The contestants were the Conservatives under Churchill and the Labour Party under Mr (Major) Attlee. It seemed that all REME work had been suspended and each Shop was holding election meetings.

Chief speaker was our Regimental Sergeant Major who, I was told early on, was a raving Communist. Now was the opportunity, he told his audiences, for the proletariat, the ordinary soldiers, to do away with the two-class system before it again entered the entire population. So Vote Labour.

In all shops the same message was going out. No longer was Churchill the War hero, he now represented the privileged class. Someone even called him a drunken bastard. Red flags were everywhere and we were commanded to VOTE LABOUR. This was a battle of Officers v Men when everyone was equal for once.

The Radio Shop, under our own Armament Sergeant Major, was busy preparing loudspeakers all over the Camp to announce the results and blackboards would be placed at strategic positions with cheerleaders. Needless to say, no Officer was visible. In any case military etiquette ruled that they would not be allowed to mix with the men. If they had appeared they would probably have been booed.

I felt this would not be an election but a rout ... did no-one support the Conservatives? So I found a blue piece of cloth and put it on a Radar Set in the yard. Within minutes it was torn down so I found another piece and awaited the day of the election results. Back in the rural parts of my native Somerset the

Conservatives held sway ... the farm workers tending to vote in sympathy with their employers. Orkney was Liberal but only a few men in Caldale were natives so that did not matter.

The results started to come in on the 26th and the final result, including the last few stragglers, on Friday 27 July. As each result came through there were rousing cheers for the Labour candidate and boos for the Conservative.

I had put my blue flag outside the Set in which I was 'working', both in rebellion to the mob rule and to add a bit of spice to the proceedings.

After the landslide to Labour had truly started, a hostile crowd gathered outside the Set and, chiefly for my own safety - although most of the barracking was good-natured - I was told to retire to the top aerial with my flag. Of course in old overalls I was not well-known to the Camp. Here, like the lookout in the crow's nest, I had a good view over much of the Camp.

After I came down for dinner I found a piece of black paper and substituted it for the blue flag. No one had one good word to say for the Conservatives and the result justified that view.

The War against Japan was still going on but the Anti-Aircraft equipment from Orkney was for a defensive position. The Radar, especially the old GLs Mark 1 and 11, were both obsolete and outdated. Many of the Radar mechanics had been posted and those who remained were mostly locals or with a bias to Natural History. We were about as wily as badgers.

I spent a lot of spare time in Kirkwall or trekking over the heaths and moors. There were film shows and the occasional concert party at the Camp.

On 6th August I was at a lecture on the works of Mozart, given by one of our Staff Sergeants, when we were interrupted for a few minutes to learn that an atomic bomb had been dropped on Hiroshima. At this moment, in the isolation of the Orkney camp, the true significance of the event escaped us. We had sensed that some new invention was 'afoot'.

Three days later the end came with the bomb on Nagasaki. The War had seemed very far away by then. A couple of us went to visit our 'family' friends in Kirwall that evening. There was rejoicing and a genuine sadness for we all realised that Orkney would become a silent place again.

At the end of August I went on two weeks' leave plus two days for both VE and VJ days. This was to be followed by a month's Agricultural Leave for me to help at home with the harvest. The German and Italian Prisoners of War helping on the farms would be returning to their battered homes.

When I returned to Caldale it was November. An elaborate system of demob
· had been worked out by the new Government to avoid putting lots of men on

156

the labour market. It was largely first in first out with penalties for younger men or bonuses for married men with families. I was group 26 and so would have to wait several months.

There was a certain amount of packing up equipment for dispatch off the Islands. I tried to disappear, and joined a colleague who was given an old maintenance hut and who undertook to mend any broken windows in the Camp. As anyone daring to

St Magnus Cathedral - Kirkwall

break a window in the gales of Orkney would have been immediately lynched, he occupied his time making small articles of ornamental furniture for his home. I was rumbled after a while and spent a few days in the newly established Education Office, then a few nights on the telephone exchange and then getting a library going.

Then in mid November when I was comfortably seated beside a red hot stove at ten o'clock one night a clerk suddenly put his head in the door. "Do you want to go on a course, Pa?" he said.

I thought all courses had ceased. "Yes!" I replied, "What sort?" - but he did not listen.

"Documents in the office first thing in the morning," he said as someone was just about to fling something at him for causing a draught.

In the Camp Office next morning I found a travel warrant with my name on it and instructions to report to Dalkeith for three weeks. The name of the Unit was a FORMATION COLLEGE at Battle Abbey. I had no idea what they taught although someone suggested I was to train as a monk. It was not REME. As usual in REME I was alone.

I caught the 'Earl of Zetland' to Scrabster and found a fellow REME character to join me in a break out from the Transit Camp into Thurso. I travelled light with a back pack and a civilian suitcase.

I had to walk some distance after leaving a bus. It was indeed an Abbey with a series of huts in the grounds. I found the Office and managed to book in. REME had not even told them I was coming and I had to explain I did not draw pay, I was a sort of honorary soldier. They gave me a hut number to find a bed space. There seemed to be a mixture of men from all branches of the Army except REME.

I hastened out across the Camp to find my hut. I had only gone a few yards when I realised I was being approached by a real Regimental Sergeant Major in

157

the full dress regalia of some Scots Regiment. "Oi! You soldier!" he called out, "Where are you going?" He was a really magnificent specimen ... even grander than any I had ever seen in Edinburgh. A real collector's item.

I sort of stumbled up to him. He was about seven feet tall. "Hut 14 - I'm told its somewhere along here."

"Stay where you are!" He marched smartly into the Office and came out with another soldier. "Show him to his hut" he commanded.

"Sorry, mate!," said my guide "He doesn't allow men to wander around looking for their huts."

When I got to the hut I got another shock as I dumped my kit. There was a spare bed either side of me. On both were the most perfectly laid out kits I have ever seen, each surmounted by a Guardsman's dress cap.

There was a large notice over the door that there would be a meeting of all personnel in the great hall at 16.00 hrs. That was in half an hour. All I could get from the lads was that the College was to train soldiers to return to civvy street. Some have a long way to go I thought.

I barely had time to do a quick survey of the Camp, chiefly to find an escape

"I think the REME man is almost there already, Sir!"

route if required. I finally got a seat at the back of the Hall and awaited events.

An Officer, dressed as a Colonel, welcomed us and it soon transpired that the College was to teach men, in three weeks, some sort of simple trade for use when they were demobbed. There would not be a great demand for professional killers in peacetime. Everyone filed out as the various classes were called. I was left sitting at the back by myself.

The Colonel saw me. "What course are you doing?" he asked. His sergeant-assistant was searching through the papers on the desk. "What Unit are you from?"

I then realised I did not know what my Unit was called; he would not accept just 'The REME lot at Caldale in the Orkneys'. I took out my documents and we finally discovered that it was 'No 245 Anti-Aircraft Workshop Company REME'. I didn't help matters by saying it was also news to me.I then had to explain I already had a job in farming. I also had an 'A' Army trade as a Telecommunications Mechanic. He said they couldn't help me much but I agreed to do a bit a carpentry just to please my Unit.

So the next morning I joined a class and had just found a nice bit of wood when an ATS girl arrived holding a piece of paper from which I gathered someone was looking for me. I was commanded to report to the Office immediately; I was, of course, accompanied there by the girl. My instructions had arrived from Caldale.

There was a less obvious part of the Camp that was, I was told, devoted to Teacher Training. Here the idea was to turn 'teachers' under the Army Education Scheme to teach elementary subjects back in the Units. So I was not going to be a monk or a carpenter.

I had my particulars again checked and I was escorted to a classroom where I found about twenty mixed rank soldiers of both sexes seated at desks, quietly chatting to themselves, and staring at a table and blackboard. I took the spare seat at the back and my neighbour told me they were awaiting the teacher. There was an air of expectancy.

After a while the door opened and a rather large Officer, wearing a Major's shoulder crown, entered the room. He beckoned us to remain seated and going up to the black board and not saying a word, drew a large red circular blob. Just as I thought he was going to go, he stopped and giving us a sort of broad welcoming smile.

"I expect for the rest of your lives most of you will remember that red circle on the board. So for our first study we are going to think about memory."

The Red Spot

The Major turned out to be an educational psychiatrist from the Education Corps and his assistant, an ex-school teacher, was a REME Radio Officer.

The morning consisted of classwork from blackboard techniques to pupil participation. We 'sat' the 11 Plus school examination and had our answers analysed. We also were individually analysed from our instant reaction to key words. Each student had to prepare a demonstration half-hour class period. I picked as my subject the digestive system of a dairy cow and described it in the block schematic diagrams so beloved by the Radar schools.

In the afternoons voluntary trips were organised for us with professional guides to Edinburgh's historical sites, power station, water works and art galleries.

We also, acting in pairs, had to devise a detailed course on our chosen subject as a final test. I found myself paired with the only other farm worker ... who happened to be a Major who had spent the War in jungle warfare with a team of mules and mountain artillery. He never gave an opinion on what he though of the likes of me although he had no use for Army class distinctions or bullshit. I suppose both of us were subject to great self discipline at both ends of soldiering.

When I returned to Caldale I was listed as a teacher of elementary maths and elementary biology. As most of the REME already had a good trade I rarely had more than two pupils and very often no one at all.

The Camp was gradually decaying for, daily, men were going down to a Camp somewhere near Edinburgh, to await demob at their home towns. Most of the senior older staff had left and there was sometimes a degree of desperation to keep the Camp running. Many men had completed mastered the art of almost continuous sleep. Each Shop still functioned as most of the equipment had to be sent down to England. (Scapa's final death warrant as a military base was 29th March 1957.) During my last six weeks I had a few unusual jobs 'just to help out'.

I did night shift on the telephone exchange and was asked to guard a prisoner at the guard hut. We spent all day in the NAAFI or in the boiler house chatting with the boilerman. I was even asked to manage the pump at the sewage works - until I threatened to reverse the motor and pump the entire contents back into the Officers' Mess as fountains in their shit house. I was never asked to do anything again.

CHAPTER TWENTYFIVE

THE JOURNEY BACK
TO CIVVY STREET

When I was forty days away from demob I decided to wear only overalls around the Camp, and to have the decreasing number chalked each morning in large figures across my back. It was now early January and the hours of daylight were short. A few men seemed to be picked off each day. Most of the older - 28-year-olds - and married men were leaving in demob groups 20, 21 and 22. I was in group 26, the largest group.

We all slept a lot as the huts were warm as coal was plentiful. Several Radio mechanics, with many months to go, were posted to the Continent, one to Greece. The Camp was slowly dying from the top down. The whole policy was to keep low activity: a sleeping man could cause no trouble.

The road to Caldale in 1994

A few wilder spirits would go drinking in the NAAFI the night before they left and seemed to get some satisfaction in exploding great chips off the huge concrete blocks, used by WW1 Airships, that straddled the Camp. They would pour fuel on one side and set light to it ... the bang sounded like a field gun.

Whenever the weather was fine I spent the day wandering in the heathland around the Camp or reading in the Kirkwall Library before visiting my 'family' in the evening.

Periodically I was required in the Camp Office to

161

complete documents for my release. Two Radio Shop members were doing the pre-release medical documents and eye tests - a chiropodist and an osteopath, whose expertise was not recognised by the Medical Corps.

I obtained the valued ABX 801 Soldier's Release Book. It contained a somewhat glowing testimonial signed by some unknown Major, which, considering my accumulated reputation, gave my entire hut a good laugh.

On the last day I said good-bye to my 'family' in Kirkwall. They had given me a delightful insight to the best of family life in the Orkneys. They knew a great deal about my life on a small farm on the far side of England. It was a strangely sad occasion and I felt humbled by their kindness to me over the previous three years.

My last duty was to write a letter to the ORCADIAN newspaper expressing my heartfelt thanks to the Islands and their residents.

The next day I was delighted to find my final journey would not be alone. Roger, who had done my medical, was going home to Bristol to resume his foot repair practice. Although I had only caught fleeting glimpses of him in the past his revolutionary attitude to military things was of a high order. We were both going straight back to civilian work.

The sea was relatively calm and we stood on the deck of the Earl of Zetland to bid the high cliffs and the Old Man of Hoy a final farewell. Our first move was to break out of the Transit Camp at Scrabster and we spent the day in cafés and at the rail terminus. Roger had a great interest in trains.

On reaching Edinburgh we decided not to report to the REME Depot but to have a week's holiday in the City. Roger arranged with the clerk that we ring up each morning to enquire if we could collect our rail warrants to proceed South. We stayed at a Red Shield (Salvation Army) Club and did a round of all the sites from the Art Galleries to the Zoo. Roger sometimes wore a civilian cap.

On 13th February 1946 we started our last, this time leisurely, train journey through Glasgow, Crewe, Birmingham and down to Bristol. I was again on my own down to Taunton where, in the Barracks where I first joined the Territorials nearly seven years previously, found No. 6 Military Dispersal Unit. Having travelled all night I claimed my last Army breakfast.

The final act was to go through the clothing store to collect a brand new civilian outfit. Civilian outfitters helped me choose a suit, overcoat, shoes and a trilby hat before I went through the 'WAY OUT' and the final gate. We emerged singly and at intervals. There was no one around to bid us good-bye, certainly no-one to say thanks. My life in the Army had just fizzled out.

Only now, when it was all over, did it really sink in to me that in the most terrible War in history, it was possible to control one's own destiny. As a loner I had found niches in the Army machine. I had volunteered for every job I did. I had always been the ferret ... never joining the rabbits. Although I had never left the lowest rank I had always received great kindness and consideration. I had nearly always managed to totally avoid

That's yer lot!

Army bullshit and indignity. Only now could I admit to myself that I had enjoyed almost every minute of my Army service.

My first job as an Artillery specialist had given me great moments on manoeuvres: watching shell fire from an observation post, driving a Bren Carrier what felt like ten thousand miles, and bird watching with the Battery range-finder. We were below the Battle of Britain in 1940. There were some interesting courses.

Then there was my extended summer holiday at the Bournemouth Municipal College in 1942, the esoteric and exciting Radar schools .... Gopsall and North Berwick, those wonderful old Radar sets ... warm, gentle, fickle yet responding to understanding and kindness. The nearest that science has ever got to re-creating the mind of a woman! One day I would marry a girl with green eyes.

I loved the Orkneys in all seasons. The aurora borealis in winter, the flowers and the birdlife. Only once did I ever really suffer from the weather ... when I was caught in a blizzard in the hills at night when I went out looking for a snowy owl. As a loner I never was a member of a team. Yet I met some delightful colleagues like ships passing in the night. They too were mostly loners. Weaving all these factors together was the unique humour that seems to pervade all adversity.

Because I had spent regular spells back on the farm I had not lost sight of my roots. I had completed an Agricultural Correspondence course in four years of the War. Farming was now ready for a post-war revolution ... the scientific developments of War would now surely be directed to peaceful purposes ... swords into ploughshares.

The rural population had changed; strange accents could be heard as one-time POWs, both German and Italian, had decided to stay on. Many of the old village men from WW1 had passed away. Gone was the wounded man with the wooden leg and 'im with the 'ook' for a hand. The farm now had no prisioners-of -war, the evacuees had gone home. Monica, the school-girl who loved talking to cows, had grown up to be a lovely young lady and was joining her parents in Paris. She had a wonderful smile and green eyes (but that is another story).

On my first full day back I retraced my path back to the top of the farm. I would have to train a new ferret to sit in my pocket but Spring my now elderly dog was at heel.

At the top gate I rested and looked back over the Axe Valley to the sea at Seaton Gap in the hazy distance. The trees in '39 had been showing the very first tinges of colour with the grass crisp from an early ground- frost. We were looking towards winter. Now the trees were bare and the grass had died back but small green shoots showed we were looking towards a spring of hope. Old Gaarge had not lived to see the peace but I remembered his last words to me "Young man," he had counselled me, "Wars are wot you make 'em."